ADDRESS

DELIVERED ON

THE CENTENNIAL ANNIVERSARY

OF THE BIRTH OF

ALEXANDER VON HUMBOLDT,

UNDER THE AUSPICES OF THE

BOSTON SOCIETY OF NATURAL HISTORY,

BY

LOUIS AGASSIZ.

WITH AN ACCOUNT OF THE EVENING RECEPTION.

BOSTON:
BOSTON SOCIETY OF NATURAL HISTORY.
1869.

ADDRESS

DELIVERED ON

THE CENTENNIAL ANNIVERSARY

OF THE BIRTH OF

ALEXANDER VON HUMBOLDT,

UNDER THE AUSPICES OF THE

BOSTON SOCIETY OF NATURAL HISTORY,

BY

LOUIS AGASSIZ.

WITH AN ACCOUNT OF THE EVENING RECEPTION.

BOSTON:
BOSTON SOCIETY OF NATURAL HISTORY.
1869.

UNIVERSITY PRESS: WELCH, BIGELOW, & CO.,
CAMBRIDGE.

ADDRESS.

Mr. President, Ladies and Gentlemen: —

I am invited to an unwonted task. Thus far I have appeared before the public only as a teacher of Natural History. To-day, for the first time in my life, I leave a field in which I am at home, to take upon myself the duties of a biographer. If I succeed at all, it will be because I so loved and honored the man whose memory brings us together.

Alexander von Humboldt was born in Berlin in 1769, — one hundred years ago this day, — in that fertile year which gave birth to Napoleon, Wellington, Canning, Cuvier, Chateaubriand, and so many other remarkable men. All America was then the property of European monarchs. The first throb of the American Revolution had not yet disturbed the relations of the mother country and her colonies. Spain held Florida, Mexico, and the greater part of South America; France owned Louisiana; and all Brazil was tributary to Portugal.

What stupendous changes have taken place since that time in the political world! Divine right of possession was then the recognized law on which governments were based. A mighty Republic has since been born, the fundamental principle of which is self-government. Progress in the intellectual world, the world of thought, has kept pace with the advance of civil liberty; reference to authority has been superseded by free inquiry; and Humboldt was one of the great leaders in this onward movement. He has bravely fought the battle for independence of thought against the tyranny of authority. No man impressed his century intellectually more powerfully, perhaps no man so powerfully as he. Therefore he is so dear to the Germans, with whom many nations unite to do him honor to-day. Nor is it alone because of what he has done for science, or for any one department of research, that we feel grateful to him, but rather because of that breadth and comprehensiveness of knowledge which lifts whole communities to higher levels of culture, and impresses itself upon the unlearned as well as upon students and scholars.

To what degree we Americans are indebted to him, no one knows who is not familiar with the history of learning and education in the last century. All the fundamental facts of popular education in physical science, beyond the merest elementary instruction, we owe to him. We are reaping daily in every school throughout this broad land, where education is the heritage even of the poorest child, the intellectual harvest sown by him. See this map of the United States; — all its important traits are based upon his investigations; for he first recognized the essential relations which unite the physical features of the globe, the laws of climate on which the whole system of isothermal lines is based, the relative height of mountain chains and tablelands, the distribution of vegetation over the whole earth. There is not a text-book of geography or a school-atlas in the hands of our children to-day which does not bear, however blurred and defaced, the impress of his great mind. But for him our geographies would be mere enumerations of localities and statistics. He first suggested the graphic methods of representing natural phenomena which are now universally adopted. The first geological sections, the first sections across an entire continent, the first averages of climate illustrated by lines, were his. Every school-boy is familiar with his methods now, but he does not know that Humboldt is his teacher. The fertilizing power of a great mind is truly wonderful; but as we travel farther from the source, it is hidden from us by the very abundance and productiveness it has caused. How few remember that the tidal lines, the present mode of registering magnetic phenomena and oceanic currents, are but the application of Humboldt's researches, and of his graphic mode of recording them!

This great man was a feeble child, and had less facility in his studies than most children. For this reason his early education was intrusted to private teachers, his parents being wealthy, and of a class whose means and position command the advantages denied to so many. It is worthy of note that when he was a little fellow not more than seven years old, his teacher was Campe, author of the German Robinson Crusoe. We can fancy how he amused the boy with the ever fresh story of Crusoe on his desert island, and inspired him even at that early age with the passionate love of travel and adventure which was to bear such fruit in later years. Neither should we omit, in recalling memories of his childhood, his tender relation to his older brother William. These two brothers, so renowned in their different departments of learning, — the elder as statesman and philologist, the younger as a student of nature, — were united from their earliest years by an intimate sympathy which grew with their growth and strengthened with their strength. They went together to the University of Frankfort, the younger being then seventeen, William nineteen. After two years at Frankfort they went to the University of Göttingen, where they passed the two following years. In these four pregnant years of student life Alexander already sketched the plans which occupied his active mind for more than threescore years and ten.

The character of the German universities is so different from ours, that a word upon his student life may not be out of place here. Untrammelled by prescription and routine, every branch of learning was open to him. Instead of being led through a prescribed course of study, an absolute freedom of selection in accordance with his natural predilections was allowed him. The effect of this is felt through his whole life; there was a universality, a comprehensiveness in his culture, which could not be obtained under a less liberal system of education.

Leaving the University at the age of twenty-one, he began to make serious preparations for the great journeys toward which all his hopes tended. Nothing has impressed me more, in reviewing Humboldt's life, than the harmony between the aspirations of his youth and the fulfilment of his riper age. A letter to Pfaff, written in his twenty-fourth year, contains the first outline of the Cosmos; its last sheets were forwarded to the publisher in his ninetieth year, two months before his death. He had thus been an original investigator for nearly seventy years.

His first journey after leaving the University was important rather for the circumstances under which it was made than for any local interest. He went to the Rhine with Georg Forster, who had accompanied Cook in his second journey round the world. He could hardly have been thrown with any one more likely to stimulate his desire to travel than this man, who had visited the South Seas, had seen the savages of the Pacific Islands, and had made valuable contributions to geographical science. Nor was this their only point of sympathy. Georg Forster was a warm republican; he had espoused the ideas of the French Revolution, and when Mayence became united to the French Republic he was sent as deputy to the National Assembly in Paris. Humboldt was too ardent and too independent to be a laggard in the great public questions of the day. Like Forster, he also believed in the Republic of France and in the dawn of civil liberty for Europe. Thus, both in political and scientific preferences, although so different in age, he and Forster were sympathetic travelling companions. This excursion was by no means a pleasure trip. Young as he was, Humboldt had knowledge enough to justify him in approaching the most difficult geological question of the day, namely, the origin of the Basalt. At that time the great war was waging between the Neptunists and Plutonists, — that is, between the two great schools in Geology, — one attributing the rocks to fire as the great constructive agent, the other asserting that all rocks were the result of water deposits. The young student brought to these subjects the truthfulness and patience which marked all his later investigations. Carried away neither by theories nor by leaders, he left in abeyance the problem which seemed to him not yet solved. His interest in this and kindred topics carried him to Freiberg, where he studied Geology with Werner, and where he made acquaintance with Leopold von Buch, who became the greatest geologist of the age, and was through life his trusted friend. He also applied himself to Anatomy and Physiology, and made physical investigations on the irritability of the muscular fibre, which he afterwards extended to the electric fishes, during his American journey.

All the while he brooded over his schemes of travel, gathering materials in every direction, in order that his mind might be prepared to understand Nature in all her aspects. His desires turned especially toward India. He wished to visit the East, and, reaching India by way of Egypt, Syria, and Persia, to cross the Pacific and return to Europe through America. In this he was foiled; but to his latest day he felt the same longing for a sight of that antique ground of civilization. At this moment all Europe was in a blaze; between contending armies there was little room for peaceful travel and investigation. We find him, therefore, floating between various plans. He went to Paris with the hope of joining Baudin's contemplated expedition to Australia. In this he was again baffled, for the breaking out of the war between France and Austria postponed the undertaking indefinitely. His next hope was Spain; he might obtain permission to visit her Transatlantic possessions and study tropical nature under the equator. Here he was successful. The scientific discoverer of America, as the Germans like to call him, was destined to start from the same shore as Christopher Columbus. He not only received permission to visit the colonies, but special facilities for his investigations were offered him.

This liberality was unexampled on the part of the Spanish government, for in those days Spain guarded her colonies with jealous exclusiveness. His enthusiasm disarmed suspicion, however, and the king cordially sustained his undertaking.

Almost ten years had passed in maturing his plans, preparing himself for their execution and obtaining the means of carrying them out. He was nearly thirty years of age when he sailed from the harbor of Corunna, running out in a dark and stormy night, and so evading the English cruisers which then blockaded the Spanish coast.

There is perhaps no part of Humboldt's life better known to the public, especially in this country, than his American journey. His fascinating "Personal Narrative" is known to all, and I need not, therefore, describe his course, or dwell upon the details of his personal experience. No period of his life, however, has had a more powerful influence upon knowledge and education than those five years of travel, and therefore I will speak at some length of their scientific results. In the very glory of his youth, and yet with an intellectual maturity which belongs to later manhood, his physical activity and endurance kept pace with the fertility and comprehensiveness of his mind. Never was the old proverbial wish, " Si jeunesse savait, si vieillesse pouvait," so near fulfilment; never were the strength of youth and the knowledge of age so closely combined.

At the first step of the journey, namely, his pause at the Canary Islands and ascension of the Peak of Teneriffe, he has left us a graphic picture of the place, of its volcanic phenomena, its geological character, and the distribution of its vegetation, in which are foreshadowed all his later generalizations. Landing in Cumana he made his first long station there. His explorations of the mountains, valleys, and sea-shore in that neighborhood, his geological researches, his astronomical observations by which the exact position of various localities was determined, his meteorological investigations, and his collections of every kind, were of vast scientific importance. He had already begun his studies upon averages of climate, the result of which, known as the "isothermal lines," was one of his most original contributions to science. With the intuition of genius he saw that the distribution of temperature obeyed certain laws. He collected, both from his own observation and from report, all that could be learned of the average temperatures in various localities, and combining all these facts he first taught geographers how to trace upon their maps those curves which give in one undulating line the varying aspects of climate upon the whole globe. His physical experiments upon animals and plants, and his collections were also of great value. At Paris he had made the acquaintance of Bonpland, a young botanist, equally determined with himself to see distant lands, who accompanied him in his journey to South America; and when Humboldt was too exclusively engaged in physical experiments to join in the botanical researches, they were nevertheless not neglected, for Bonpland was unremitting in the study of plants and in making collections.

After months thus spent in the neighborhood of the coast, Humboldt crossed the Llanos, the great plains which divide the basin of the Orinoco from the sea-shore. Here again every step of his journey is marked by original research. He has turned those desert plains into enchanted land by the power of his thought, and left us descriptions, as fascinating from their beauty as they are valuable for their novelty and precision. In his long and painful journey through the valley of the Orinoco he traced the singular network of rivers by which this great stream connects, through the Cassiquiare and the Rio Negro, with the Amazons, — a fresh-water route which is, no doubt, yet to become one of the highways of the world. Had it not been for the illiberality of the Portuguese government, he would probably have gone down the Rio Negro to the Amazons, and would perhaps have changed completely the course which he ultimately took. He was, however, turned back from the mighty river by a prohibition which made it dangerous to proceed farther on pain of imprisonment and the possible renunciation of all his cherished plans. When, in my late exploration of the Amazonian Valley, I read his narrative again, on the spot, I could not but contrast the cordial liberality which smoothed every difficulty in my path with the dangers, obstacles, and suffering which beset his. I approached, however, so near the scene of his labors that I was constantly able to compare my results with his, and to recognize the extent of his knowledge and the comprehensiveness of his views, even where the progress of science led to a different interpretation of the facts.

I omit all notice of his visit to Cuba, and his journey through Mexico, interesting as they were, remarking only that to him we owe the first accurate maps of those regions. So imperfect were those published before him, that even towards the close of the last century the position of Mexico differed by about three hundred miles in the maps published by different geographers. Humboldt's is the first general map of Mexico and Cuba based upon astronomical observations.

The next great stage of the American journey is along the ridge of the Andes. There is a picturesque charm about this part of the undertaking which is irresistible. At that time travelling in those mountains was infinitely more difficult than it is now. We follow him with his train of mules, bearing the most delicate instruments, the most precious scientific apparatus, through the passes of the great chain Measuring the mountains, — sounding the valleys as he went, — tracing the distribution of vegetation on slopes 20,000 feet high, — examining extinct and active volcanoes, — collecting and drawing animals and plants, — he brought away an incredible amount of information which has since filtered into all our scientific records, remodelled popular education, and become the common property of the civilized world. Many of these ascensions were attended with infinite danger and difficulty. He climbed the Chimborazo to a height of 18,000 feet at a time when no other man had ever ascended so far above the level of the sea, and was only prevented from reaching the summit by an impassable chasm, in which he nearly lost his life. When, a few years later, Gay-Lussac made his famous ascent in a balloon, for the sake of studying atmospheric phenomena, he rose only 1,200 feet higher.* Returning from the Andes, Humboldt skirted the Pacific from Truxillo to Acapulco, and paused in Mexico again. There he ascended all the great mountains in the neighborhood, continuing and completing the same investigations which he had pursued with such persistency through his whole laborious journey. He studied volcanic action, mines, the production of precious metals, their influence upon civilization and commerce, latitudes and longitudes, averages of climate, relative heights of mountains, distribution of vegetation, astronomical and meteorological phenomena. From Mexico he went to Havana, and from Havana sailed for Philadelphia. His stay in this country was short. He was cordially received by Jefferson on his visit to Washington, and warmly welcomed by scientific men in Philadelphia. But he made no important re-

* The ascension of Mont Blanc by De Saussure was the only exploit of that kind on record before. Even as late as 1842 the ascent of the Jungfrau attracted some attention. Nowadays tourists may run up the highest summits of the Alps to drink the health of their friends.

searches in the United States, and sailed for Europe soon after his arrival.

He returned to Paris in 1804, having been five years absent from Europe. It was a brilliant period in science, letters, and politics in the great capital. The Republic was still in existence; the throes of the Revolution were over, and the reaction toward monarchical ideas had not yet culminated in the Empire. Laplace, Gay-Lussac, Cuvier, Desfontaines, Delambre, Oltmanns, Fourcroy, Berthollet, Biot, Dolomieu, Lamarck, and Lacépède were leaders then in the learned world. The young traveller, bringing intellectual and material treasures even to men who had grown old in research, was welcomed by all, and in this great centre of social and intellectual life he made his home for the most part, from 1805 to 1827; from the last days of the Republic, through the rise and fall of the Empire, to the restoration of the Bourbons. He devoted himself to the publication of his results, and secured as his collaborators in this work the ablest men of the day. Cuvier, Latreille, and Valenciennes worked up the zoölogical collections, Bonpland and Kunth directed the publication of the botanical treasures, Oltmanns undertook the reduction of the astronomical and barometrical observations, while he himself jointly with Gay-Lussac and Provençal made investigations upon the respiration of fishes and upon the chemical constitution of the atmosphere and the composition of water, which have left their mark in the annals of chemistry. While of course superintending more or less all the publications, Humboldt himself was engaged especially with those upon physical geography, meteorology, and geology. The mere enumeration of the volumes resulting from this great expedition is impressive. It embraces three folio volumes of geographical, physical, and botanical maps, including scenery, antiquities, and the aboriginal races; twelve quarto volumes of letter-press, three of which contain the personal narrative, two are devoted to New Spain, two to Cuba, two to zoölogy and comparative anatomy, two to astronomy, and one to a physical description of the tropics. The botanical results of the journey occupy not less than thirteen folio volumes, ornamented with magnificent colored plates. As all these works are in our Public Library in Boston, I would invite my hearers to a real intellectual treat and a gratification of their æsthetic tastes, in urging them to devote some leisure hour to turning over the leaves of these magnificent volumes. A walk through the hot-houses of the largest botanical garden — and unfortunately we have no such on this continent — could hardly be more impressive than an examination of these beautiful plates. Add to these a special work on the position of rocks in the two hemispheres, one on the isothermal lines, his innumerable smaller papers, and lastly, five volumes on the history of geography and the progress of nautical astronomy during the fifteenth and sixteenth centuries, more or less directly connected with Humboldt's own journey, though published in later years. His investigations into the history of the discovery of America have a special interest for us. We learn from him that the name of our continent was first introduced into the learned world by Waltzeemüller, a German professor, settled at St. Didié, in Lorraine, — Hylacomylus, as he called himself, at a time when scholars were wont to translate their names into the dead languages, and thought it more dignified to appear under a Greek or Latin garb. This cosmographer published the first map of the New World, with an account of the journeys of Americus Vespucci, whose name he affixed to the lands recently discovered. Humboldt shows us, also, that Columbus's discovery was no accident, but grew naturally out of the speculations of the time, themselves the echo of a far-off dream, which he follows back into the dimness of Grecian antiquity. We recognize again here the characteristic features of Humboldt's mind, in his constant endeavor to trace discoveries through all the stages of their progress.

Although he made his head-quarters in Paris, it became necessary for Humboldt, during the preparation of so many extensive works, to undertake journeys in various parts of Europe; to examine and re-examine Vesuvius, and compare its mode of action, its geological constitution, and the phenomena of its eruptions with what he had seen of the volcanoes of South America. On one of these occasions he ascended Vesuvius in company with Gay-Lussac and Leopold von Buch. That single excursion, undertaken by such men, was fruitful in valuable additions to knowledge. At other times he went to consult rare books in the great libraries of Germany and England, or to discuss with his brother in Berlin, or with trusted friends in other parts of Europe, the work in which he was engaged, comparing notes, assisting at new experiments, suggesting further inquiries, ever active, ever inventive, ever suggestive, ever fertile in resource, — neither disturbed by the great political commotions which he witnessed, nor tempted from his engrossing labors by the most brilliant offers of public service or exalted position. It was during one of his first visits to Berlin, where he went to consult about the organization of the University with his brother William, then minister of state in Prussia, that he published those fascinating "Views of Nature," in which he has given pictures of the tropics as vivid and as exciting to the imagination as if they lived on the canvas of some great artist.

The question naturally arises, Who provided for the expenses of these extensive literary undertakings? — Humboldt himself. No one knows exactly what he has spent in the publication of his works. Some approach to an estimate may, however, be made by computing the cost of printing, paper, and engraving, which cannot have amounted to less than two hundred and fifty thousand dollars. No doubt the sale indemnified him in some degree, but all know that such publications do not pay. The price of a single copy of the complete work on America is two thousand dollars, — double that of the great national work published by France upon Egypt, for the publication of which the government spent about eight hundred thousand dollars. Of course very few copies can be sold of a work of this magnitude.

But from his youth upward Humboldt spent his private means liberally, not only for the carrying out and subsequent publication of his own scientific undertakings, but to forward the work of younger and poorer men. The consequence was that in old age he lived upon a small pension granted to him by the King of Prussia.

His many-sidedness was remarkable. He touched life at all points. He was the friend of artists, no less than of scientific and literary men. His desire to make his illustrations worthy of the great objects they were to represent brought him into constant and intimate relation with the draughtsmen and painters of his day. Even David did not think it below his dignity to draw an allegoric title-page for the great work. He valued equally the society of intelligent and cultivated women, such as Madame de Staël, Madame Récamier, Rahel, Bettina, and many others less known to fame. He was intimate with statesmen, politicians, and men of the world. Indeed, the familiarity of Humboldt with the natural resources of the countries he had visited, — with their mineral products and precious metals, — made his opinion valuable not only in matters of commerce, but important also to the governments of Europe; and after the colonies of South America had achieved their independence, the allied powers of Europe invited him to make a report upon the political condition of the new republics. In 1822 he attended the Congress of Verona, and visited the South of Italy with the King of Prussia. Thus his life was associated with the political growth and independence of the New World, as it was intimately allied with the literary, scientific, and artistic interests of the Old. He never, however, took an active part in politics at home, and yet all Germany looked upon him as identified with the aspirations of the liberal party, of which his brother William was the most prominent representative.

Before closing this period of Humboldt's life I would add a few words more in detail upon the works published by him after his return from South America. One of the first fruits in the rich harvest reaped from this expedition was the successful attempt to which I have already alluded at representing graphically the physical features of that continent. Thus far such representations had mainly consisted in maps and the delineation of the characteristic plants and animals. Humboldt devised a new method, equally impressive to the eye and comprehensive in its outlines. Impressed by the fact that vegetation changes its character as it ascends upon the side of high mountains, — thus presenting successive terraces upon their slopes, — he conceived the idea, already suggested by his examination of the Peak of Teneriffe, of drawing upon the outline of a conical mountain the different aspects of its surface from the level of the sea to its highest peak. Thus he could exhibit at a glance all those successive zones of vegetation, represented upon the diagram before you, and drawn by him at Guayaquil in 1803. It is copied from his work on the physical aspect of the tropics and the geographical distribution of plants. (Explanations from the diagram.) Afterwards he extended these comparisons to the temperate and arctic zones, and ascertained that, as we proceed further north, the gradation of the vegetation, at the level of the ocean, corresponds to its succession upon mountain slopes, — until, towards the Arctics, it assumes a remarkable resemblance to the plants found near the line of perpetual snows under the Tropics. But this is not all. The intervening expanse from North to South, as far as the equator, and then in reverse order to the Antarctic regions, also exhibits, in proportion to the elevation of the land, a vegetation characterized by intermediate forms.

In the same way he reproduced the general

appearance of the inequalities of the earth's surface by drawing ideal sections across the regions described. In the first place, through Spain, afterwards from La Guayra to Caraccas across the Cumbre, from Carthagena to Santa Fé de Bogota, and finally through the whole continent of America, from Acapulco to Vera Cruz (as represented in another diagram before you). And this not by mere approximations, but founding his profiles upon his own barometric and astronomical observations, which he multiplied to such an extent that his works are to this day the chief source of information concerning the physical geography of the regions visited by him.

Not satisfied with this, he undertook to represent, in like manner, the internal structure of the earth, by drawing similar charts upon which the relative position of the rocks, with signs to indicate their mineralogical character, is faithfully portrayed. The first chart of this kind was drawn by him in Mexico in 1804, and presented to the School of Mines of that city. It was afterwards published in the Atlas of the American Journey. — We are thus indebted to him for the whole of that graphic method which has made it possible to delineate, in visible outlines, the true characteristics of physical phenomena; for afterwards this method was applied to the representation of the oceanic currents, the direction of the prevalent winds, the tidal waves, the rise and fall of our lakes and rivers, the amount of rain falling upon different parts of the earth's surface, the magnetic phenomena, the lines of equal average temperature, the relative height of our plains, table-lands and mountain chains, their internal structure, and the distribution of plants and animals. Even the characteristic features of the History of Mankind are now tabulated in the same way upon our ethnographical maps, in which the distribution of the races, the highways of navigation and commerce, the difference among men as to language, culture, creeds, nay, even the records of our census, the estimates of the wealth of nations, down to the statistics of agriculture and the averages of virtue and vice, are represented. In short, every branch of mental activity has been vivified by this process, and has undergone an entire transformation under its influence.

His paper upon the isothermal lines was published in the "Mémoires de la Société d'Arcueil," a scientific club to which, in the beginning of this century, the most eminent men of the age belonged. Though a mere sketch, the first delineation of the curves uniting different points of the earth's surface which possess the same average annual temperature under varying latitudes, exhibits already the characteristic features of these lines, which myriads of observations of a later date have only confirmed. No other series of investigations shows, more plainly than this, to what accurate results an observer may arrive, who understands how to weigh critically the meaning of his facts however few they may be. (This other diagram before you represents the isothermal lines as contrasted with the degrees of latitude.)

The barometrical and astronomical observations upon which his numerous maps are based were computed and reduced to their final form by his friend Oltmanns. They fill two large quarto volumes, and amount to the accurate determination of nearly one thousand localities. They are not taken at random, but embrace points of the highest importance, with reference to the geographical distribution of plants and animals and the range of agricultural products. Humboldt has himself added an introduction to this work in which he gives an account of the instruments used in his observations and the methods pursued by him in his experiments, and discusses the astronomical refractions in the torrid zone.

Thus the physical geography of our days is based upon Humboldt's investigations. He is, indeed, the founder of Comparative Geography, that all-embracing science of our globe, unfolded with a master hand by Karl Ritter, and which has now its ablest representative in our own Guyot, the author of the maps before you. His correspondence with Berghaus testifies his intense interest in the progress of geographical knowledge. To Humboldt this world of ours is indeed not only the abode of man, it is a growth in the history of the Universe, shaped according to laws, by a long process of successive changes, which have resulted in its present configuration with its mutually dependent features. The work upon the Position of Rocks in the two hemispheres tells the history of that growth as it could be told in 1823, and is of course full of gross anachronisms; but at the same time it exhibits the wonderful power of generalization and combination which Humboldt possessed,—as, for instance, where he says in few beautiful words, fertile in consequences not yet fully appreciated by the naturalists of our day: "When we examine the solid mass of our planet, we perceive that the simple minerals are found in associations which are everywhere the same, and that the rocks do not vary, as organized beings do, according to the differences of latitude or the isothermal lines under which they occur"; thus contrasting in one single phrase the whole organic world with the inorganic in their essential character. In practical geology we owe to him the first recognition of the Jurassic formation. It was he who introduced into our science those happy expressions, "geological horizon" and "independence of geological formations." He also paved the way for Elie de Beaumont's determination of the relative age of mountain chains by his discussion upon the direction of stratified rocks and by the parallels he drew between the age of plutonic and sedimentary formations; nor had it escaped him that distant floræ and faunæ, though of the same age, may be entirely different.

The collection of zoölogical and anatomical papers, in two quarto volumes, with numerous colored plates, is full of valuable contributions to the Natural History of Animals, from his own pen, as well as that of his collaborators. The most remarkable are his description of the Condor, which must have delighted the French zoölogists, who could not fail to compare it with the glowing pages of their own Buffon; his Synopsis of the South American Monkeys, rivalling the works of Audebert and Geoffroy

St. Hilaire; his account of the Electric Eel and the Catfish thrown out by the burning volcanoes of the Andes, contrasted with the Great Natural History of Fishes by Lacépède; his paper on the respiration of Crocodiles and the larynx of Birds and Crocodiles, daring upon his own ground the greatest anatomist of the age, the immortal Cuvier. Indeed, it must have created a profound sensation in the learned world when a naturalist, all whose previous publications related to physical subjects, suddenly came forward as a master among masters in the treatment of zoölogical and anatomical questions.

The botanical works have appeared under several titles. We have first the "Plantes Équinoxiales" in two folio volumes, with 140 plates, by Bonpland; the monograph of the Mélastomacées and that of the Rhéxiées, in two folio volumes, with 120 plates, also by Bonpland; then the Mimosées by Kunth, in one folio volume, with 60 plates; the revision of the Graminées, in one folio volume, with 220 plates, by Kunth; and finally the "Nova Genera et species Plantarum" by Kunth, in seven folio volumes, with 700 plates. Altogether thirteen folio volumes, with 1240 plates, most of which are beautifully colored, and remain unsurpassed for fidelity of description and fulness of illustration. Though the descriptive part of these splendid volumes is from the pen of his fellow-traveller Bonpland, and his younger friend Kunth, it would be a mistake to suppose that Humboldt had no share in their preparation. Not only did he assiduously collect specimens during the journey, but it was he who made, on the spot, from the living plant, drawings and analyses of the most remarkable and characteristic trees; the general aspect of which could not be preserved in the specimens gathered for the herbarium. Besides this there are entire chapters concerning the geographical distribution of the most remarkable families of plants, their properties, their uses, &c., entirely written by Humboldt himself. It was he, also, who for the first time divided the areas of the regions he had explored into botanical provinces, according to their natural physical features; thus distinguishing the Flora of New Andalusia and Venezuela from that of the Orinoco basin, that of New Granada, that of Quito, that of the Peruvian Andes, and those of Mexico and Cuba. It was he, also, who first showed that the whole Vegetable Kingdom contains, after all, but a few distinct types, which characterize the vegetable carpet of the earth's surface, in different parts of the world, under different latitudes and at different heights. He closes one of these expositions with a few words, which I cannot pass by without quoting. "Such investigations," he says, "afford an intellectual enjoyment and foster a moral strength which fortify us against misfortunes, and which no human power can overcome."

In 1827, at the urgent solicitation of his brother, Humboldt transferred his residence from Paris to Berlin. With this step there opens a new phase in his life. Thus far he had been absolutely independent of public or official position. Conducting his researches as a private individual, if he appeared before the public at all, it was only in reading his papers to learned Academies. Now he began to lecture in the University. In his first course, consisting of sixty-one lectures, he sketched the physical history of the world in its broadest outlines, — it was, in truth, the programme of the Cosmos. Since I shall give an analysis of this work in its fitting place, I will say nothing of the lectures here, except that, as a teacher, he combined immense knowledge with simplicity of expression, avoiding all technicalities not absolutely essential to the subject.

In the midst of his lectures there came to him an invitation from the Russian government to visit the Russian provinces of Asia. Nothing could be more gratifying to a scientific man than the terms in which this proposition was made. It was expressly stipulated by the Emperor that he wished the material advantages which might accrue from the expedition to be a secondary consideration. Humboldt was to make scientific research and the advancement of knowledge his first aim, and he might turn his steps in whatever direction he chose. Never before had any government organized an expedition with so little regard to purely utilitarian considerations.

This second great journey of Humboldt is connected with a hope and disappointment of my own. I was then a student in Munich. That University had opened under the most brilliant auspices. Almost every name on the list of professors was also prominent in some department of science or literature. They were not men who taught from text-books or even read lectures made from extracts of original works. They were themselves original investigators, daily contributing to the sum of human knowledge. Martius, Oken, Döllinger, Schelling, Fr. von Baader, Wagler, Zuccarini, Fuchs, Vogel, von Kobell, were our teachers. And they were not only our teachers but our friends. The best spirit prevailed among the professors and students. We were often the companions of their walks, often present at their discussions, and when we met for conversation or to give lectures among ourselves, as we constantly did, our professors were often among our listeners, cheering and stimulating us in all our efforts after independent research.

My room was our meeting-place, — bedroom, study, museum, library, lecture-room, fencing-room, — all in one. Students and professors used to call it the little Academy. Here Schimper and Braun for the first time discussed the laws of phyllotaxis, that marvellous rhythmical arrangement of the leaves in plants which our great mathematician in Cambridge has found to agree with the periods of the rotation of our planets. Among their listeners were Professors Martius and Zuccarini; and even Robert Brown, while in Munich, during a journey through Germany, sought the acquaintance of these young botanists. Here for the first time did Michahelles lay before us the results of his exploration of the Adriatic and adjoining regions. Here Born exhibited his wonderful preparations of the anatomy of the Lamper-Eel. Here Rudolphi made us acquainted with his exploration of the Bavarian Alps and the shores of the Baltic. These my fellow-students in Munich were a bright, promising set, — boys then in age, many of whom did not live to make their names famous in the annals of science. It was in our little Academy that Döllinger, the great master in physiology and embryology, showed to us, his students, before he had even given them to the scientific world, his wonderful preparations exhibiting the vessels of the villosities of the alimentary canal; and here he taught us the use of the microscope in embryological investigation. And here also the great German anatomist, Meckel, came to see my collection of fish skeletons, of which he had heard from Döllinger. Such associations, of course, made us acquainted with everything of importance which was going on in the scientific world. The preparations of Humboldt for his Asiatic journey excited our deepest interest, and I was filled with a passionate desire to accompany the expedition as an assistant.

General La Harpe, then residing in Lausanne, who had been the preceptor of both the Emperors Alexander and Nicholas of Russia, and who knew Humboldt personally, was a friend of my family, and he wrote to Humboldt in my behalf, asking that I might join the expedition as an assistant. But it was not to be. The preparations for the journey were already made, and Ehrenberg and Gustav Rose, then professors at the University of Berlin, were to be his travelling companions. I should not mention the incident here, but that, slight as it was, it marks the beginning of my personal relation with Humboldt.

The incidents of Humboldt's Asiatic journey are less known to the public at large than those of his longer American ramblings. Short as it was, however, — for he was absent only nine months, — he brought to the undertaking such an amount of collateral knowledge, that its scientific results are of the utmost importance, and may be considered as the culmination of his mature research and comprehensiveness of views. His success was insured also by the ample preparations of the Russian government, orders having been given along the whole route to grant him every facility. Descending the Volga to Kasan, and hence crossing to Ikaterinenburg over the Ural Mountains, he passed through Tobolsk on the Irtish, to Barnaul on the Obi, and reached the Altai Mountains on the borders of China, thus penetrating into the heart of Asia. His researches into the physical constitution of what was considered the high table-land of Asia revealed the true features of that vast range of mountains. Touched by his cultivated genius, the most insignificant facts became fruitful, and gave him at once a clew to the real character of the land. The presence of fruit-trees and other plants, belonging to families not known to occur in elevated regions, led him to distrust the existence of an unbroken, high, cold table-land, extending over the whole of Central Asia, and by a diligent comparison of all existing documents on the subject, combined with his own observations, he showed that four great parallel mountain ridges, separated by gradually higher and higher level grounds, extend in an east-westerly direction. First, the Altai, bordering on the plains of Siberia, from the northern slope of which descend all the great rivers flowing into the Arctic Ocean, — as the Irtisch with the Obi, the Jenisei and the Lena; then the Thian-Shan, south of the plateau of Soongaria; next, the Kuenlun, south of the plateau of Tartary; finally, the Himalaya range, separating the plateau of Thibet from the plains of the Ganges. He showed also the connection of the Himalaya Mountains through the Hindoo-koo and the Demavend with the far-off range of the Caucasus. These east-westerly ranges, giving form and character to the continent of Asia, are then contrasted with the north-southerly direction of the Ghauts, the Soliman and Bolor range, and the

Ural Mountains which divide Europe from Asia. Approaching the great highways, over which the caravans of the East, from Delhi and Lahore, reach the northern marts of Samarcand, Bokhara, and Orenburg, he opens to us the most striking vistas of the early communication between the Aryan civilization and the Western lands lying then in the darkness of savage life. He inquired also into the course of the old Oxus, and the former channels between Lake Aral and the Caspian Sea. The level of that great inland salt lake, about two or three hundred feet lower than the surface of the sea, suggested to him its former communication with the Arctic Ocean, when the Steppes of the Kirghis formed an open gulf and the northern waters poured over those extensive plains. After examining the German settlements about the Caspian Sea, he returned to St. Petersburg by way of Orenburg and Moscow.

The scientific results of this journey are recorded in two separate works, the first of which, under the title of "Asiatic Fragments of Climatology and Geology," is chiefly devoted to an account of the inland volcanoes which he had had an opportunity of studying during this journey. He had now examined the volcanic phenomena upon three continents, and had gained an insight more penetrating and more comprehensive than was possessed by any other geologist into their deep connection with all the changes our globe has undergone. Volcanoes were no longer to him mere local manifestations of a limited focus of eruption; he perceived their relation to earthquakes and to all the phenomena coincident with the formation of the inequalities of the earth's surface.

The contrast between the Siberian winter and the great fertility of the neighborhood of Astracan, where he found the finest vineyards he had ever seen, led him to consider anew the causes of the irregularities of temperature under corresponding latitudes, and thus to enlarge his knowledge of the isothermal lines, which he had first sketched in his younger years, and the rationale of which he now clearly set forth. In one comprehensive view he showed the connection between the rotation of the earth, the radiation of its surface, the currents of the ocean, and especially among the latter the Gulf Stream, in their combined influence upon conditions of temperature, producing under identical latitudes such contrasts of climate as exist between Boston, Madrid, Naples, Constantinople, Tiflis on the Caucasus, Hakodadi in Japan, and that part of our own coast in California, where stands the city which bears his own venerated name.

The second work relating to the Asiatic journey appeared under the title of "Central Asia," being an account of his researches into the mountain systems and the climate of that continent. The broadest generalizations relating to the physics of the globe, showing Humboldt's wonderful familiarity with all its external features, are here introduced in a short paper upon the average elevation of the continents above the level of the sea, as compared with the average depths of the ocean. Laplace, the great geometer, had already considered the subject; but Humboldt brought to the discussion an amount of facts which showed conclusively that the purely mathematical consideration of the inquiry, as handled by Laplace, had been premature. Taking separately into consideration the space occupied upon the earth's surface by mountain ridges with that occupied by high table-lands, and the far more extensive tracts of low plains, Humboldt showed that the average elevation of the earth, estimated by Laplace at more than one thousand metres, could in fact be scarcely one third that amount,— a great deal less, indeed, than the average depth of the sea.

In 1830, after his return to Berlin, he was chosen as the fitting messenger from one great nation to another. The Restoration which followed the downfall of Napoleon had been overturned by the July revolution, and Humboldt who had lived through the glory of the Republic and the most brilliant days of the Empire was appointed by the King of Prussia to carry an official greeting to Louis Philippe and the new dynasty. He had indeed the most friendly relations with the Orleans family, and was, from private as well as public considerations, a suitable ambassador on this occasion.

Paris had greatly changed since his return from his first great journey. Many of those who had made the glory of the Academy of Sciences, in the beginning of the century, had passed away, and a new generation had come up. Elie de Beaumont, Dufrénoy, the younger Brongniart, Adrien de Jussieu, Isidore Geoffroy, Milne Edwards, Audouin, Flourens, Guillemain, Pouillet, Duperrey, Babinet, Decaisne, and others, had risen to distinction, while the older Ampère, the older Brongniart, Valenciennes, De Blainville, Arago and Geoffroy St. Hilaire had come forward as leaders in science. Cuvier, just the age of Humboldt himself, was still active and ardent in research. His salon, frequented by statesmen, scholars, and artists, was, at the same time, the gathering-place of all the most original thinkers in Paris; and the pleasure of those delightful meetings was unclouded, for none dreamed how soon they were to end forever, — how soon that bright and vivid mind was to pass away from among us.

In those days a fierce discussion was carried on before the Academy as well as in public lectures. Goethe had declared the unity of structure in the bony frame of all the Vertebrates, and had laid the foundation of the morphology of plants. These new views had awakened the interests and passions of the whole world of science to a degree hitherto unknown in her peaceful halls. Cuvier, strange to say, had taken ground in opposition to Goethe's views upon the Vertebrate type, while Geoffroy St. Hilaire, a devoted adherent of Goethe's ideas, had expressed his convictions in words not always courteous toward Cuvier. The latter had retorted with an overwhelming display of special knowledge, under which the brilliant generalizations of St. Hilaire seemed to be crushed. Cuvier was then giving a course of lectures in the Collége de France on the history of science, into which he wove with passionate animation his objections to the new doctrine. Humboldt attended these lectures regularly, and I had frequently the pleasure of sitting by his side and being the recipient of his passing criticism. While he was impressed by the objections of the master-anatomist, he could not conceal his sympathy for the conception of the great poet, his countryman. Seeing more clearly than Cuvier himself the logic of his investigations, in whispered comments during the lectures, he constantly declared that whatever deficiencies the doctrine of unity might still contain, it must be essentially true, and Cuvier ought to be its expounder instead of its opponent. The great French naturalist did not live to complete these lectures, but the view expressed by his friend was prophetic. Cuvier's own researches, especially those bearing upon the characteristics of the four different plans of structure of the animal kingdom, have helped to prove, in his own despite, though in a modified form, the truth of the doctrine he so bitterly opposed.

The life which Humboldt now led was less exclusively that of a student than it had been during his former Paris life. He was the ambassador of a foreign court. His official position and his rank in society, as well as his great celebrity, made him everywhere a cherished guest, and Humboldt had the gift of making himself ubiquitous. He was as familiar with the gossip of the fashionable and dramatic world as with the higher walks of life and the abstruse researches of science. He had at this time two residences in Paris, — his lodging at the Hôtel des Princes, where he saw the great world, and his working-room in the Rue de la Harpe, where he received with less formality his scientific friends. It is with the latter place I associate him; for there it was my privilege to visit him frequently. There he gave me leave to come to talk with him about my work and consult him in my difficulties. I am unwilling to speak of myself on this occasion, and yet I do not know how else I can do justice to one of the most beautiful sides of Humboldt's character. His sympathy for all young students of nature was one of the noblest traits of his long life. It may truly be said that toward the close of his career there was hardly one prominent or aspiring scientific man in the world who was not under some obligation to him. His sympathy touched not only the work of those in whom he was interested, but extended also to their material wants and embarrassments. At this period I was twenty-four; he was sixty-two. I had recently taken my degree as Doctor of Medicine, and was struggling not only for a scientific position, but

for the means of existence also. I have said
that he gave me permission to come as often
as I pleased to his room, opening to me freely
the inestimable advantages which intercourse with
such a man gave to a young investigator like
myself. But he did far more than this. Occupied and surrounded as he was, he sought me
out in my own lodging. The first visit he paid
me at my narrow quarters in the Quartier Latin,
where I occupied a small room in the Hôtel du
Jardin des Plantes, was characteristic of the man.
After a cordial greeting, he walked straight to what
was then my library, — a small book-shelf containing a few classics, the meanest editions bought
for a trifle along the quays, some works on philosophy and history, chemistry and physics, his
own Views of Nature, Aristotle's Zoölogy, Linnæus's
Systema Naturæ, in several editions, Cuvier's
Règne Animal, and quite a number of manuscript
quartos, copies which, with the assistance of my
brother, I had made of works I was too poor
to buy, though they cost but a few francs a
volume. Most conspicuous of all were twelve
volumes of the new German Cyclopædia presented
to me by the publisher. I shall never forget,
after his look of mingled interest and surprise at
my little collection, his half-sarcastic question as
he pounced upon the great Encyclopædia, — "Was

machen Sie denn mit dieser Eselsbrücke?" What are you doing with this *ass's bridge?* — the somewhat contemptuous name given in Germany to similar compilations. "I have not had time," I said, "to study the original sources of learning, and I need a prompt and easy answer to a thousand questions I have as yet no other means of solving."

It was no doubt apparent to him that I was not over familiar with the good things of this world, for I shortly afterward received an invitation to meet him at six o'clock in the Galerie vitrée of the Palais Royal, whence he led me into one of those restaurants, the tempting windows of which I had occasionally passed by. When we were seated, he half laughingly, half inquiringly asked me whether I would order the dinner. I declined the invitation, saying that we should fare better if he would take the trouble. And for three hours, which passed like a dream, I had him all to myself. How he examined me, and how much I learned in that short time! How to work, what to do, and what to avoid; how to live; how to distribute my time; what methods of study to pursue, — these were the things of which he talked to me on that delightful evening. I do not mention this trivial incident without feeling that it may seem too familiar for the occasion; nor should I give it at all, except that it shows the sweetness and kindliness of Humboldt's nature. It was not enough for him to cheer and stimulate the student; he cared also to give a rare indulgence to a young man who could allow himself few luxuries.

The last period of his life was spent in Berlin, and while there to the end of his long and laborious career he was engaged with the publication of his Cosmos, and also in editing the great work, on the Kavi language, left by his brother William, who died in 1835. Besides these important undertakings, he was unceasingly engaged in fostering magnetic observations and the establishment of magnetic observatories. He likewise felt a lively interest in the proposed interoceanic Canal between the Atlantic and Pacific Oceans, the lines for which he had carefully considered in earlier years. Surrounded by loving and admiring friends, covered with honors and distinctions, these days were rich in peaceful enjoyment.

One of the most prominent features of Humboldt's mind, as philosopher and student of nature, consists in the keenness with which he perceives the most remote relations of the phenomena under consideration, and the felicity with which he combines his facts so as to draw the most comprehensive pictures. This faculty is more particularly exhibited in the Cosmos, the crowning effort of his mature life. With a grasp transcending the most profound generalizations of the philosophers of all ages, he draws at first in broad outlines a sketch of the whole Universe. With an eye sharpened by the most improved instruments of the Observatory, and exalted by the experience of all his predecessors, he penetrates into the remotest recesses of space, to seek for the faintest ray of light that may furnish any information concerning the expanse of the heavenly vault and the age of the celestial bodies. He thus makes the rapidity with which light is propagated a measure of the distance which separates the visible parts of the whole system from one another, as well as a means of approximately estimating the duration of their existence. He next considers the various appearances of the celestial bodies, the different kinds of nebulæ, their form and relations to one another and to the so-called fixed stars; describes in graphic and fascinating language the landscape-like loveliness of their combinations in the Milky-Way and the various constellations ; discusses the nature of the double-stars, and, gradually approaching our own system by a comparison of our sun to other suns, rises, by a sublime effort of the imagination, to a conception of the form of their united systems in space. In the description of our solar system one might have expected an exposition similar to the methods adopted by astronomers; but the object of our great physicist is not to write a synopsis of Astronomy. He plunges without hesitation into the earliest history of the formation of our earth, the better to illustrate the relations to one another of the sun and the planets with their satellites, the comets, and the hosts of meteors of all kinds which come flashing, like luminous showers, through the atmosphere. Our globe is reviewed in its turn. First, its structure, the density of its mass, in the estimation of which the oscillations of the pendulum become a plummet-line with which to fathom the inapproachable deep; then the volcanoes are made to reveal the everlasting conflict between the interior caldrons of melted materials and the consolidation of the ruffled surface ; the distribution of heat and light, the climates, as depending upon the inequalities of form and relief, the currents of the ocean, as modifying the temperature, the magnetic phenomena, the aurora borealis, the shooting stars, etc., are discussed in turn. The changes which our globe has undergone in course of ages are next described : how the lands gradually rose above the level of the sea ; how they first formed disconnected archipelagos; how mountains grew up in succession, and their relative age ; the form and extent of successively larger continental islands, their plants and animals ; — nothing escaped his attention ; everything is represented in its true place and relation to the whole. Especially attractive are his delineations of the distribution of plants and animals upon the present surface of the earth, of which an account has already been given.

This mode of treating his subjects, emphatically his own, has led many specialists to underrate Humboldt's familiarity with different branches of science; as if knowledge could only be recorded in pedantic forms and a set phraseology.

But Humboldt is not only an observer, not only a physicist, a geographer, a geologist of matchless power and erudition, he knows that nature has its attraction for the soul of man; that, however uncultivated, man is impressed by the great phenomena amid which he lives; that he is dependent for his comforts and the progress of civilization upon the world that surrounds him. This leads to an appreciative analysis of the enjoyment derived from the contemplation of nature, and to considerations of the highest order respecting the influence which natural highways have had upon the races of men, in their distribution upon the whole surface of the globe.

In speaking of his later days I cannot omit some allusion to a painful fact connected with his residence at Berlin. The publication of a private correspondence between Varnhagen von Ense and Humboldt has led to many unfriendly criticisms upon the latter. He has been blamed for holding his place at court, while, in private, he criticised and even satirized severely everything connected with it. It is not easy to place one's self in the right point of view with reference to these confidential letters. It must be remembered that Humboldt was a Republican at heart. His most intimate friends, from Forster, in his early youth, to Arago, in his mature years, were ardent Republicans. He shared their enthusiasm for the establishment of self-government among men. An anecdote preserved to us by Lieber shows that he did not conceal his sympathies, even before the King who honored him so highly. Lieber, who was present at the conversation, gives the following account of it: "The King of Prussia, Humboldt, and Niebuhr were talking of the affairs of the day, and the latter spoke in no flattering terms of the political views and antecedents of Arago, who, it is well known, was a very advanced Republican of the Gallican School, an uncompromising French democrat. Frederic William the Third simply abominated Republicanism; yet when Niebuhr had finished, Humboldt said, with a sweetness which I vividly remember: "Still this monster is the dearest friend I have in France."

Can we, therefore, be surprised that, in his confidential letters to a sympathizing friend, he should not refrain from expressing his dislike of the petty intrigues and low sentiments which he met among courtiers. I received, myself, a letter from Humboldt, written in the days when the reactionary movements were at their height in Prussia, in which, in a strain of deep sadness and despondency, he expresses his regret at the turn political affairs had taken in Europe, and his disappointment at the failure of those aspirations for freedom with which he had felt the deepest sympathy in his youth. We may wish that this great man had been wholly consistent, that no shadow had rested upon the loyalty of his character, that he had not accepted the friendship and affection of a King whose court he did not respect and whose weaknesses he keenly felt. But let us remember that his official station there gave him the means of influencing culture and education in his native country in a way which he could not otherwise have done, and that in this respect he made the noblest use of his position. His sympathy with the oppressed in every land was profound. We see it in his feeling for the aborigines in South America, in his abhorrence of slavery. I believe that he would have experienced one of the purest and deepest joys of his life had he lived to hear of the abolition of slavery in the United States. His dislike of all subserviency and flattery, whether toward himself or others, was always openly expressed, and was unquestionably genuine.

The philosophical views of Humboldt, his position with reference to the gravest and most important questions concerning man's destiny, and the origin of all things, have been often discussed, and the most opposite opinions have been expressed respecting them by men who seem equally competent to appreciate the meaning of his writings. The modern school of Atheists claims him as their leader; as such we find him represented by Burmeister in his scientific letters. Others bring forward his sympathy with Christian culture as evidence of his adherence to Christianity in its broadest sense. It is difficult to find in Humboldt's own writings any clew to the exact nature of his convictions. He had too great regard for truth, and he knew too well the Aryan origin of the traditions collected by the Jews, to give his countenance to any creed based upon them. Indeed, it was one of his aims to free our civilization from the pressure of Jewish tradition; but it is impossible to become familiar with his writings without feeling that, if Humboldt was not a believer, he was no scoffer. A reverential spirit for everything great and good breathes through all his pages. Like a true philosopher, he knew that the time had not yet come for a scientific investigation into the origin of all things. Before he attempted to discuss the direct action of a Creator in bringing about the present condition of the Universe, he knew that the physical laws which govern the material world must be first understood; that it would be a mistake to ascribe to the agency of a Supreme Power occurrences and phenomena which could be deduced from the continued agency of natural causes. Until some limit to the action of these causes has been found, there is no place, in a scientific discussion, as such, for the consideration of the intervention of a Creator.

In the closing paragraph of the first volume of the Cosmos Humboldt distinctly objects to the consideration of the sphere of intelligence in connection with the study of Nature. But the time is fast approaching, and indeed some daring thinkers have actually entered upon the question, — Where is the line between the inevitable action of law and the intervention of a higher power? where is the limit? And here we find the most opposite views propounded. There are those who affirm that, inasmuch as force and matter are found to be a sufficient ground for so many physical phenomena, we are justified in assuming that the whole universe, including organic life, has no further origin. To these, I venture to say, Humboldt did not belong. He had too logical a mind to assume that an harmoniously combined whole could be the result of accidental occurrences. In the few instances where, in his works, he uses the name of God, it appears plainly that he believes in a Creator as the lawgiver and primary originator of all things. There are two passages in his writings especially significant in this respect. In the second volume of the Cosmos, when speaking of the impression man receives from the contemplation of the physical world, he calls nature God's majestic realm, — "Gottes erhabenes Reich." In his allusion to the fearful catastrophe of Carracas, destroyed by an earthquake in 1812, the critical inquirer may even infer that Humboldt believed in a special Providence. For he says with much feeling: "Our friends are no more, the house we lived in is a pile of ruins; the city I have described no longer exists. The day had been very hot, the air was calm, the sky without a cloud. It was Holy Thursday; the people were mostly assembled in the churches. Nothing seemed to foreshadow the threatening misfortune. Suddenly, at four o'clock in the afternoon, the bells which were struck mute that day began to toll. It was the hand of God, and not the hand of man, which rang that funeral dirge." In his own words: "Es war Gottes, nicht Menschenhand, die hier zum Grabgeläute zwang."

One word more before I close. I have appeared before you as the representative of the Boston Natural History Society. It was their proposition to celebrate this memorable anniversary. I feel grateful for their invitation, for the honor they have done me. I feel still more grateful for the generous impulse which has prompted them to connect a Humboldt scholarship, as a memorial of this occasion, with the Museum of Comparative Zoölogy at Cambridge. I trust this token of good-will may only be another expression of that emulation for progress which I earnestly hope may forever be the only rivalry between these kindred institutions and their younger sister in Salem. We have all a great task to perform. It should be our effort, as far as it lies in our power, to raise the standard of culture of our people, as Humboldt has elevated that of the world. May the community at large feel with equal keenness the importance of each step now taken for the expansion, in every direction, of all the means of the highest culture. The physical suffering of humanity, the wants of the poor, the craving of the hungry and naked, appeal to the sympathy of every one who has a human heart. But there are necessities which only the destitute student knows; there is a hunger and thirst which only the highest charity can understand and relieve, and on this solemn occasion let me say that every dollar given for higher education, in whatever special department of knowledge, is likely to have a greater influence upon the future character of our nation than even the thousands and hundreds of thousands and millions which have already been spent and are daily spending to raise the many to material ease and comfort.

In the hope of this coming golden age, let us rejoice together that Humboldt's name will be permanently connected with education and learning in this country, with the prospects and institutions of which he felt so deep and so affectionate a sympathy.

PRAYER

BY THE

Rev. JAMES WALKER, D.D.,

OFFERED PREVIOUS TO THE ADDRESS BY PROFESSOR AGASSIZ.

O THOU infinite Source of life and light, we invoke thy blessing on these services in the memories they awaken and the hopes they inspire. We acknowledge and adore that providence by which gifted men are raised up from time to time to make us better acquainted with the heavens which declare thy glory and with the earth which shows thy handiwork. Impress it, we beseech thee, upon the great masters of science that they also are prophets, set to reveal the thoughts and the ways of the living God. Suffer not the rapid increase of natural light to dazzle our eyes, or obscure or confuse that divine light which comes from thy Word and from the instincts and aspirations of the human soul; so that science and faith may reverently work together for the good of man and the glory of God, through Christ our Lord. Amen.

DURING the address by Professor Agassiz every available place in the Music Hall was occupied. Delegates were present from the leading literary and scientific societies throughout New England. The colleges of Yale and Brown, Bowdoin and Dartmouth, were represented; so also was Harvard University, by its President and Faculties. On the part of the Commonwealth was his Excellency Governor Claflin; while his Honor the Mayor of Boston, and delegates from both branches of the City Government, were officially present.

The Music, noble and effective, and in every way worthy the occasion, was under the conductorship of Mr. Carl Zerrahn, who gave his valuable services, as did also the Orpheus Musical Society, aided by various other German Musical Associations.

Mr. J. K. Paine presided at the organ, rendering Bach's wonderful Toccata in F in a masterly manner. This was followed by the beautiful "Hymn to Music" by Lachner, with all its variety and richness of melody, together with grand selections from Beethoven and Mozart; while the exquisite four-part song by Mendelssohn ("Wenn Gott will rechte Gunst erweisen"), both in music and words, was peculiarly appropriate: —

> "To whom God special favor grants,
> Him sends he out into the world,
> Shows him the wonders of creation,
> In mountain and forest, stream and field."

THE EVENING RECEPTION.

COMMITTEE OF ARRANGEMENTS.

R. C. WATERSTON,   N. B. SHURTLEFF,
JEFFRIES WYMAN,   SAMUEL KNEELAND,
SAMUEL H. SCUDDER.

THE EVENING RECEPTION.

IN the evening a large and distinguished audience assembled at Horticultural Hall. Invited guests and delegates from literary and scientific societies, members of both branches of the City Government, gentlemen of the School Board, and others interested in the cause of Education, were present, representing every State in New England, as well as more distant parts of the country.

Around the Hall various interesting mementos of Humboldt were displayed. Upon the platform were two portraits (which were also at the Music Hall during the delivery of Professor Agassiz's address), — one painted at Mexico in 1803 by a Spanish artist, and placed at the disposal of the Committee of Arrangements by Mr. Wm. F. Poole, late librarian of the Boston Athenæum; the other painted at Berlin by Mr. Wight when Humboldt had reached the age of eighty-three. The latter portrait was lent for the occasion by the artist. There was also a palm-branch, borne on the coffin of Humboldt at his funeral, which was brought from Berlin as a gift to Professor Agassiz, together with the pen with which the illustrious naturalist had last written. Before the desk was a large chromo-lithograph, representing Humboldt in his study, lent for the occasion by Mr. Charles Deane, Secretary of the Historical Society. A remarkably fine proof-plate of one of the best engravings of Humboldt, obtained at Berlin by Professor Young, was upon one side of the Hall, and upon the other a life-like photograph of Humboldt, presented by himself to Professor Brown. Several original notes and letters to artists and scholars attracted much attention, among which were three autograph papers belonging to the Chairman, — Alexander von Humboldt's between that of Cuvier and Sir Isaac Newton.

The Rev. R. C. Waterston, as Chairman of the Committee of Arrangements, presided. In his opening remarks he welcomed the delegates of the different literary and scientific societies who were present, expressing his congratulations at the great success which had attended the celebration. A brief statement followed respecting the Humboldt Scholarship. It had been the desire of the Committee that the occasion should not be one of mere pleasure, even though of high intellectual gratification, but that it should result in a substantial memorial, which, while it was a fitting monument to the memory of Humboldt, would also prove an aid and encouragement to worthy students in their preparatory studies; for this end a "Scholarship" had been proposed, to be associated with the names of Humboldt and Agassiz, and to be forever devoted to the aid of students of Natural History in the Museum of Comparative Zoölogy at Cambridge. The Chairman was happy in being able to state that, aside from the proceeds at the Music Hall, the sum of over five thousand dollars had been subscribed as the foundation of a permanent fund; the proposed scholarship was therefore secured. After this gratifying statement, which was received with hearty applause, the Chairman called upon Colonel Thomas Wentworth Higginson, of Newport, R. I., who responded as follows: —

He expressed his pleasure at the fact that the Committee had made this occasion a festival not alone for the scientific societies of Massachusetts, but of New England, thus uniting the sympathy of that larger Massachusetts of which Boston is still the centre. In collecting subscriptions a ready response had been shown from New England men whose lives had been spent far from their birthplace, as in California or Ohio. There was something in the name of Humboldt that appealed to all Americans, not alone for his explorations of this continent, but because his name represented the comprehensiveness of culture, which ought to be, though it is not yet, American. In that superficiality of training which yet prevails among us, where any man who can use a microscope ranks as a *savant*, and every one who remembers his Greek alphabet is called a scholar, we need such commemorations as this. What touched us all to-day in Professor Agassiz's address was its personal passages, — the tribute of one great scientific leader to another; and the best thing that any one of us can do to-night is to say simply what he owes to Humboldt, as the best evidence of the intellectual reach of that remarkable man.

Many of us owe to our early readings of Humboldt our first impressions of what a comprehensive scholarship should be. He took some things from us indeed, and dispelled some pleasing illusions. Through him we learned with regret that monkeys did not, as we had been told, construct Pacific railways with each other's tails and run express-trains across rivers by their aid. We learned, too, that if a man wished to commit *felo de se*, no vampire-bat would ever aid in his intentions, since these alarming animals rarely bite, and their bite never kills. But the wonders which he took away were trifling beside the more genuine wonders that he told.

Then those of us whose vocation was Literature discovered with delight that Humboldt was not a mere scientist, but one who loved beauty in nature and in art, and always recognized that side of culture. He said in his "Cosmos" that under free institutions no single branch of knowledge would be pursued to the exclusion of others. All were precious, he said, whether they yielded physical wealth, or whether, more permanent in their nature, they transmitted in the works of mind the glory of nations to remotest posterity. The Spartans, he added, notwithstanding their Doric austerity, prayed the gods to grant them the beautiful with the good.

So wide was Humboldt's mind, it has been said that if he had not been a man of science, he would have been an artist or a poet. This is hardly probable, for though he had the appreciation of beauty, the love of constructive form was not strong in him. Still he has left some fine poetic statements, as where he says, in his correspondence: "A book about external nature should produce on us the same impression as nature itself," or when he says that "a diamond is a pebble arrived at consciousness." And even if this last phrase is only a satire on Schelling, it is none the less poetic.

It is fortunate for great men that one of the annoyances to which they are least liable is that of being present at their own centennial anniversary. Fontenelle might have done this,—he who at the age of one hundred apologized for not stooping to pick up a lady's fan with the agility he had possessed at eighty,—" *Ah, que n'ai-je plus mes quatre-vingt ans!*" But certainly Humboldt, with his views of old age, would not have wished to rival Fontenelle; and the best wish that can be offered for the *savants* of this Boston Natural History Society is that each of them may deserve to have his hundredth birthday celebrated, and that no one of them may have the ill luck to survive till that occasion.

Rev. Frederic H. Hedge, D. D. was then introduced, and spoke as follows:—

Mr. Chairman,—It is hard gleaning in a field in which Agassiz has been with his sickle. But since you call upon me, I will say that the thing which most impressed me, as I listened to the discourse this afternoon, was the psychological marvel of such a nature as Humboldt's, and the illustration it affords of the capabilities of the human mind. Here was a man whose inappeasable greed of knowledge had appropriated all the science of his time, who knew all that was known in his day of things below and things above. The word " Cosmos," the title he gave to his immortal work, is an apt designation of the mind of the author,—a mind in which the universe mirrored itself in all its vastness and all its minuteness, with its infinitely great and its no less amazing infinitely little. Where shall we look for the parallel and peer of such a mind? To find his match we have to go back two thousand years. We cannot stop at the name of Laplace or of Buffon; these men were great in single provinces of science, but Humboldt was great in all. We cannot stop at Newton or Leibnitz, though Newton seems to have gravitated with a more absolute *aplomb* to the truth of fact, and though Leibnitz pierced with a finer *aperçu* to the heart of things. We cannot stop at Bacon, whose merit is not to have found, nor even to have sought with sincerity, but only to have taught men what and how to seek. We cannot stop till we come to Aristotle. And here we have an even parallel. Between Humboldt and Aristotle there are, it seems to me, some points of striking resemblance. Both of these sages mastered and extended the science of their time, — with this difference in favor of the Greek, that he explored the realm of ideas as well as of things; with this difference in favor of the German, that the science of things and their relations — cosmic science — was a thousand-fold more complex and difficult in the nineteenth century of the Christian era than in the fourth of the ante-Christian. Both were fortunate in being partakers of the recent stimulus given by a great philosophic movement, — that of Socrates in the one case, in the other that of Kant. Both were contemporaries of great world-conquerors and shared the impulse imparted to their time, — the one by Alexander, the other by Napoleon the First.

Dante called Aristotle "*il maestro di color' che sanno,*" — master among them that know. And what better title can be conferred upon Humboldt? Master among them that know, — the master *savant*.

Another thing which fills my soul with profound admiration when I think of Humboldt is the heroism of his life, — a life which exceeded in breadth as well as in length the ordinary limits of mortality. I admire his loyal devotion to the single aim of extending the area of the human mind. I admire the indomitable enterprise which ransacked the globe in search of materials with which to build his monumental Cosmos. I admire no less the indefatigable industry which methodized and shaped those materials for after ages. A new standard of the possibilities of a single life is given in what he was and what he did. There was no senescence in his experience. He passed away in the midst of tasks which the noon of his life bequeathed to its evening, and which the evening did not seek to escape. And when he died it seemed as if the civilized world, from the Himalaya to the Andes, sighed in sympathy with the going down of a man who carried a universe in the lobes of his brain, and who counted an ally and a friend wherever nature had a student or science a home.

One thing more. The Professor has told us of the service which Humboldt rendered to humanity by freeing men from the pressure of Jewish tradition. I accept the statement. From all that was puerile and inadequate in Jewish or Jew-Christian theology he was free himself, and helped to make others free. But the central truth of Judaism, the truth of Semitic monotheism, was as true to him as to any before or since. An impression went abroad at the time of his death that Humboldt was an atheist. We all know how loosely, how unthinkingly, that term is applied. That he did not receive the anthropomorphism of the vulgar conception I can well suppose. But that he rejected the idea of a conscious Intelligence at the heart of the world — that Intelligence which all his life was spent in tracing — nothing shall convince me, not even an unguarded saying of his own. For I am persuaded that without the belief in such an Intelligence, and a purpose and a method corresponding therewith, he would not have had the heart to prosecute his inquiries. For what use or instruction, or what satisfaction would there be in observing and classifying material phenomena, if those phenomena represented no order and obeyed no law? And when we say " Order," Mr. Chairman, and when we say " Law," we say God. And when we affirm the constancy of that order and the certainty of that law, we bear witness of one at least of the attributes of Deity, — his unchangeable veracity. Those stated processes which make the life of nature and which Humboldt so loved to note, — the stars in their courses, the ever-recurring phases of earth and sky, precession of equinoxes, succession of seasons, gravitation, magnetism, — these are Nature's comment on the text of the Spirit, " God is true." And when Humboldt applied the methods he had learned in academic Europe and the laws announced by students of nature in other centuries, — applied these to the measurement of mountains on the other side of the globe, knowing them to be as apt and applicable then as in all past time, he unwittingly confessed his belief in a God whose " truth endureth through all generations."

But if, after all, it should prove to be the case — if that were possible which I deny — that the greatest scientist of modern time, in his search after truth, had missed the first and most essential of all truths, — the being of God, — what then? Why then I should say that the man himself is the most convincing proof of the truth he missed. I should feel that the marvel of such a mind, a wonder surpassing any of those it explored, must have had its adequate cause; that the finite intelligence which looked creation through presupposes an infinite Intelligence as its origin and ground. The highest mortal can only be explained as the product of a more than mortal Power.

Mr. Ralph Waldo Emerson, in response to a call from the Chairman, spoke to this effect: —

He was reluctant to speak, but felt a cordial sympathy in this day's wide celebration of the memory of a man who had knit the continents together. He had this afternoon heard the delightful discourse in praise of Humboldt. Our eminent Professor had never delivered a discourse more wise, more happy, or of more varied power. The subject was worthy of him. Humboldt was one of those wonders of the world, like Aristotle, like Julius Cæsar, like the admirable Crichton, who appear from time to time, as if to show us the possibilities of the human mind, the force and the range of the faculties,—a universal man, not only possessed of great particular talents, but they were symmetrical; his parts were well put together. As we know, a man's natural powers are often a sort of committee that slowly, one at a time, give their attention and action; but Humboldt's were all united, one electric chain, so that a university, a whole French Academy, travelled in his shoes. With great propriety, he named his sketch of the results of science "Cosmos." There is no other such survey or surveyor. The wonderful Humboldt, with his solid centre and expanded wings, marches like an army, gathering all things as he goes. How he reaches from science to science, from law to law, folding away moons and asteroids and solar systems in the clauses and parentheses of his encyclopædic paragraphs! There is no book like it, none indicating such a battalion of powers. You could not put him on any sea or shore, but his instant recollection of every other sea or shore illuminated this. He was properly a man of the world; you could not lose him; you could not detain him; you could not disappoint him, for at any point on land or sea he found the objects of his researches. When he was stopped in Spain and could not get away, he turned round and interpreted their mountain system, explaining the past history of the continent of Europe. He belonged to that wonderful German nation, the foremost scholars in all history, who surpass all others in industry, space, and endurance. A German reads a literature whilst we are reading a book. One of their writers warns his countrymen that 't is not the Battle of Leipsic, but the Leipsic-Fair Catalogue, which raises them above the French. I remember that Cuvier tells us of fossil elephants; that Germany has furnished the greatest number; — not because there are more elephants in Germany, — O no; but because in that empire there is no canton without some well-informed person capable of making researches and publishing interesting results. I know that we have been accustomed to think they were too good scholars, that because they reflect they never resolve, that " in a crisis no plan-maker was to be found in the empire "; but we have lived to see now, for the second time in the history of Prussia, a Statesman of the first class, with a clear head and an inflexible will.

Professor E. J. Young was next called upon, and made the following remarks, introducing interesting autographic letters from Humboldt: —

I have been asked to give some personal recollections of the great man who has been honored throughout the world to-day. Everything is of interest that relates to him who commanded, not only the esteem and reverence, but the affection of all who knew him; and his name is deservedly dear to all Americans, for he felt the deepest interest in our country, and he was always the firm supporter of liberal principles.

It is from a sense of personal obligation and gratitude, as one who was privileged to share in his universal benevolence, that I am prompted to speak of him. Being in Berlin during the Christmas holidays in 1854, and having a letter of introduction, I called, with a friend and fellow-countryman, for the purpose of seeing him. He lived in a plain, unpretending house in Oranienburger Strasse. We rang the bell, when the outer door opened, and we ascended the staircase to the second story, where we saw his name upon the door. We rang again here, when an attendant appeared, and we inquired if his "Excellency" was at home. This was the title by which he was addressed, which had been conferred upon him by the King when he made him one of his Privy Councillors. We were conducted into his library, which is so familiar to all through the well-known prints, and then we entered his study, which was a small room with a table, a green-covered sofa, maps upon the wall, and books and papers lying about. Presently he came in and greeted us very cordially. His frame was slightly bent, his head was silvered, but his eye beamed with its wonted brightness. We could not but feel a certain awe in presence of the man who had laid the world under such obligations to him, whose name was a household word in both hemispheres, and who, in a city distinguished for its great men, was the foremost of them all. There was, however, a benignity on his countenance and an affableness in his manner, that removed all restraint and made us feel perfectly at home.

He at once addressed us in English, and spoke with great animation, fluency, and rapidity. The conversation turned upon English literature, and he alluded to several authors, and surprised us by his familiarity with them. He spoke of himself, and said that he was accustomed to work till midnight, when he took a few hours' sleep, and then began his work again. He expressed much dissatisfaction at the ecclesiastical and political reaction that was then going on, with which he had not the least sympathy. He had great contempt for all time-servers and trimmers; and an anecdote is told of him that on one occasion he called a visitor's attention to a chameleon which had been lately sent to him, saying: " This creature has the remarkable faculty of being able to turn one eye up to heaven, while he keeps the other on the earth. Many church officers can do the same." He referred to our own country, and gave utterance to his abhorrence of the system of slavery, while he mentioned with peculiar interest the Free States, showing himself to be, as he said he was, " half an American." We could not but be surprised and delighted to hear these words at that time from one who was the friend of the King and the chief ornament of his court. Humboldt never disguised his adherence to the liberal party, and he was even called a French Jacobin because of his democratic principles. As we were about to leave, he pointed to a striking statuette of Immanuel Kant, remarking particularly upon his figure and dress, and expressing great admiration for his character.

What impressed me most in this interview was the vivacity, freshness, and enthusiasm of the venerable man, — for he was then eighty-five years of age, — and at the same time the grace and courtesy which marked all his movements. He listened with the closest attention to our words, and his conversation was marked by that geniality of spirit which gives such a charm to all his writings. I came away grateful for the privilege which I had enjoyed of conversing with the most eminent man of the century, and feeling that it was worth a voyage across the Atlantic to have seen him.

In the following year, being engaged in translating an elaborate History of German Philosophy, and well knowing the difficulties and discouragements — growing out of the popular impression in regard to the tendency of such studies — which must be encountered, I obtained from some of the most distinguished theologians and philosophers certain testimonials which I proposed to print in a Prospectus, hoping thus to be able to publish the work. Remembering the kindness with which I had been received by Baron Humboldt, and his interest in our country, I ventured to write to him, stating my plans and asking if he was disposed to append any remarks in regard to this study, considering it from his own point of view. He at once wrote to me a most cordial letter, in which he says: —

"Erdmann's History of Philosophy is well calculated to remove objections, to stimulate mental activity, and to benefit also the physical sciences, by leading to a reflective study of the phenomena which are given to us by experience. I gladly promise you not only a recommendation, but a warm appeal to those in America who look with favor upon my own writings. I add a request, that if the antediluvian old man does not send what he promises during the week before your departure, you will simply send me word, 'I leave Halle on such a day.' I am very particular in regard to matters which I consider important."

After a few days the paper came. Omitting what is said of the original and the translation, it is, rendered into English, as follows: —

"The author and the translator are not unaware that a certain prejudice against German Philosophy, originating in ignorance of the subject and in misunderstanding of its religious bearings, prevails in many countries, and especially in the Free States of North America, where scientific culture has made such excellent and already fruitful progress. Mental freedom is far more difficult to acquire than political freedom, and the forms of the latter sometimes pave the way but slowly to the attainment of the former. Tendencies which are unfavorable to an unrestricted freedom of inquiry, and which attempt to shut out from it certain regions of the world of thought, are productive of injury, inasmuch as by so doing they cause narrowness of view even in regard to those subjects where it is permitted.

"With the wholly objective tendency of my mind, which has been induced by travel and a very checkered life; with my simple endeavor to discover the laws which connect natural phenomena as the results of experimental science, my works can make no claim to the rank of a rational (or speculative) science of nature. Having turned aside from the path of pure philosophical speculation, by which my never-to-be-forgotten brother, William von Humboldt, gave strength and brilliancy alike to his æsthetic writings as well as to his treatise upon the structure of languages, I feel myself called to warmly recommend the present work in consequence of the deep respect which in my long career I have always expressed in favor of philosophical research, and the inspiring influence which it has exerted on the whole science of nature; and I have been opposed only to the perversion of man's noble faculties, when it has resulted in a dogmatic and contracted Philosophy of Nature, which fancied itself perfect.

"The increase of philosophical studies is especially the need of an age in which the gigantic advances of the mechanical and chemical sciences are giving such a favorable impulse to the industrial pursuits of nations, and when at the same time the general desire to obtain information which may be readily applied within very narrow spheres — growing out of the division of productive labor — threatens to keep men from aspiring after higher knowledge and a broader range of thought. The seeking after what is useful for material ends, which is irresistible and praiseworthy in itself, does not retard the intellectual life of nations (as experience shows), when along with it an interest is fostered for those studies which enrich the mind with logically connected ideas, and call forth the ennobling images of creative fancy.

"The translation of German philosophical works into a language which is extended over a large portion of the earth, and, unhindered in its diffusion, will soon occupy a still greater area, has an importance which cannot be overestimated, since whatever relates to the differences in the races of men, to their division into species, and to the organic structure of languages, cannot be successfully investigated or portrayed without a knowledge of what profound thinkers have already explored. A considerable part of the material which travellers have collected is almost useless for Ethnography and Comparative Philology, because the collectors have been deficient in leading ideas. In both sections of the New World, and wherever English and North American ships penetrate, a wide field lies open for observation. What German, Danish, English, and North American missionaries have already done most creditably and intelligently in this respect, is not ignored in this general statement.

"In thus bringing together the various considerations which give a manifold importance to this difficult and valuable undertaking, I believe that, in recommending a book so weighty and instructive, I can appeal with confidence to those in the New World who retain a friendly recollection of my own labors.

"ALEXANDER VON HUMBOLDT.
"Potsdam, 2 June, 1855."

This paper was accompanied by the following note, in German: —

"BERLIN, 3 June, 1855. In the night.

"I hope, dear sir, that this somewhat too hastily written fragment will come at the right time into your hands. The returning illness of the King had drawn me to Potsdam, whence I have returned this evening. Since I possess no copy of this, I beg you speedily to inform me that it has come safely into your hands. Where I say that mental freedom is more difficult to attain than political freedom, I might have cited the fanaticism of the Protestants of Geneva and Holland.

"I enclose a warm recommendation to Bunsen, whose name in England stands higher than almost any other German name. Show him my *opus*, however, in a clear copy, which I am unable to send you; since, although from twenty-five hundred to three thousand letters circulate every year from my hand, I have an abhorrence of all private secretaries."

I have read these papers, which have never been made public before, because they show the *man*, — his kindness of heart, his liberal spirit, his interest in true culture and in the intellectual development of our country. I need not say how deeply I was moved on receiving them, and that I prize them among my choicest treasures. It seems to me that they contain most timely words, which are worthy of being considered by our people, especially now when the study of Philosophy is beginning to receive more attention, and a new course of lectures is to be devoted to it in our own University. They testify also to the breadth and largeness of that mind, which could appreciate the value of what might have been thought foreign to his pursuits, but to which no department of learning was foreign or unimportant. His knowledge was universal. He was a monarch in the realm of science. And no king ever received more loyalty and devotion than were paid to him. He needed no rank or title. He had the voluntary homage of all classes. But his real crown was his character. He was as remarkable for his genial, kindly, disinterested qualities, as he was for his intellectual gifts. There was in him that beautiful blending of dignity and simplicity, of learning and modesty, of genius, liberality, goodness, and grace, which constitutes true greatness. This has caused him to be idolized by his countrymen, and to be honored by the world.

The Chairman stated that an order had been given to Mr. Wight (the artist who painted from life the portrait of Humboldt) to execute an exact copy of that painting. This work would now be unveiled, and if it should prove in every respect satisfactory, the Chairman would take great pleasure in presenting it, on this centennial anniversary, to the Boston Society of Natural History.

The covering was removed, and, standing there upon the artist's easel, the resemblance was so perfect to the original portrait which stood by its side, as to call forth spontaneous applause.

In connection with the portrait the artist had written the following interesting account of Humboldt: —

"REV. R. C. WATERSTON: —

"Dear Sir, — You have requested me to give some account of Humboldt, whose portrait I had the honor to paint. I beg leave briefly to state that in 1852 I saw him in Berlin. He was at that time eighty-three years of age. The first interview was on the occasion of his sitting for the portrait in February of that year. I found him a man rather below the medium stature, dressed with the utmost simplicity, in black. His step was moderate, but firm and decided, with his head a little inclined forward. In conversation his face would glow with enthusiasm, and his small clear eyes sparkle with animation. He was apparently very tenacious of his time. There were five sittings. I found him always prompt to the minute. Knowing that he had received several decorations from crowned heads, I asked him if he wished me to represent any of them in his portrait; he replied that he preferred it should be painted without any ornament whatever. He spoke of his pleasant visit to the United States, and took great interest in the affairs of our country. At his house he showed me several pencil drawings of mountain scenery made by his own hand, very carefully done, and as carefully preserved.

"My studio was in Franzosisch Strasse. His residence was in another part of the city, where he lived in a plain, substantial building, in a quiet and unostentatious manner. As soon as it became known that a portrait was being painted of Humboldt, a lively interest was manifested upon the subject, particularly among the American residents and students, an unusually large number of whom were at that season in Berlin. On each sitting he was accompanied by a valet, who attended him up stairs, and either left or remained in the hall until the allotted time for sitting within expired, when Humboldt immediately arose, and, politely taking his leave, departed. An interesting conversation was kept up at intervals during the sittings, at two or three of which the Hon. Theo. S. Fay, our Chargé d'Affaires in Prussia, was present. When the portrait of the great naturalist was completed, many persons, citizens and strangers, as well as artists, and among the latter Cornelius, famed for his magnificent cartoons and frescos in church, palace, and cathedral, and Rauch, the immortal sculptor and author of the statue of Frederick the Great, together with other personal friends of Humboldt, came to see it. Before the portrait was sent to America it was exhibited to the citizens in the grand hall of the Art Union of Berlin.

"It affords me great pleasure to place in your hands the original portrait of Humboldt, to be used on this occasion of the centennial celebration of his birth. The copy of the portrait which you desired is now completed. I consider it as faithful a likeness, in every respect, as the original.

"Very respectfully, your obedient servant,
"M. WIGHT.
"Boston, Sept. 8, 1869."

Accompanying the above was an autograph note of Humboldt addressed to the artist, which was also presented by the Chairman to the Natural History Society.

Dr. Charles T. Jackson, Vice-President of the Society, accepted in its behalf the portrait of Humboldt with expression of thanks. Humboldt himself had declared the original portrait by Wight the best of himself ever painted; and all present would see that this copy by the same artist resembled the original as much as possible.

He compared the painting with a very fine photograph, presented to the Society this day by Mrs. D. Jay Browne, in which every one might notice how perfectly the expression of Humboldt had been caught by Mr. Wight in his picture.

Dr. Jackson then related some personal reminiscences of Humboldt, whom he often met in Paris in 1830, at Cuvier's Lectures on the History of the Natural Sciences, at the Academy of Sciences, at General La Fayette's, and at Baron Ferrusac's soirées.

He remarked that the materials collected by Humboldt in Mexico had not been exhausted in 1830, for he heard him read several papers on the physical geography and geology of Mexico at the Academy, where he was listened to with the most earnest attention by that illustrious assembly. It was amusing to see how Cuvier managed to prevent M. Geoffroy St. Hilaire from making his communications on his favorite theme of Transcendental Anatomy by calling for a valuable communication from Humboldt the moment he saw Geoffroy preparing to speak, while the great popularity of Humboldt was sure to cause the President to call upon him to address the Academy. Humboldt was all the time unconscious of the fact that he was interfering with the communications of the illustrious comparative anatomist. Cuvier was strongly opposed to Geoffroy St. Hilaire's theories.

The power of prediction in matters of science has always attracted the attention of mankind. Murchison has great credit for predicting the gold in Australia long before it was actually discovered. He judged from the geological character of the rocks of that country, specimens of which had been brought to England. Humboldt had also this happy scientific power, and, from the law of association of minerals, predicted the discovery of diamonds and platinum in the United States. He wrote to Professor Tellkampf, "Diamonds and platinum must be found in the gold deposits of the United States (see my work on the Ural Mountains). I have asked for years if they have been found, and nobody will answer me." Professor Tellkampf placed this letter in the hands of Dr. Jackson, who read it at the next meeting of the American Society of Geologists and Naturalists, and a committee was appointed to investigate the matter. At the next year's meeting of that Society diamonds were reported to be found in the Georgia, North Carolina, and Virginia gold deposits, and in 1850 platinum was found in the placers of California by Mr. George O. Barnes, a pupil of Dr. Jackson, and a sample of it was sent to Humboldt. So his prophecy was fufillled.

Dr. Jackson next called attention to Humboldt's preparations for his scientific travels, as a good suggestion to young travellers who wish to accomplish the largest possible amount of work. Humboldt served a regular apprenticeship in learning how to make the best observations and to collect and preserve all objects of Natural History, before he set forth on his journey to Mexico and South America. From the astronomer he learned how to obtain faultless elements for the determination of latitude and longitude. He likewise learned how to make the best geodesic measurements, how to observe meteorological phenomena, and make the proper records. From the taxidermist and botanist he learned the manner of preparing his collections of animals and plants; from the arboriculturist, how to make roots grow on the branch of an adult tree, so that he could bring home a fruit-bearing part of it that would thrive in the green-houses of Europe. So thorough was Humboldt's training that he was able to sweep the whole field of science in his travels. He was a thorough mineralogist and geologist, — a pupil of the illustrious Werner. He studied chemistry and physics with Gay-Lussac, Thénard, Biot, and Arago in France; and thus this many-sided scientist was one of the most, if not the most competent observer that ever set forth to explore the works of nature in a new field for science.

There may be specialists greater in their particular departments than Humboldt; but for grand views, universal grasp, and comprehensive generalizations, Humboldt was never equalled and probably will never be surpassed. His love for America and American institutions, and his kindness to such of our fellow-countrymen as had the honor of meeting him, is known to all.

The chairman remarked, that, looking upon the many eminent men by whom he was surrounded, all of whom it would be a privilege to hear, he felt embarrassed by the very affluence of riches. But time in its flight was inexorable, and in the present instance courtesy was specially due to the city in which we had assembled, whose official representatives favored us this evening by their presence, as they had also in the afternoon at the Music Hall. He therefore would call upon his Honor the Mayor.

Mayor Shurtleff, in responding, said that after the eloquent addresses already made it would not be expected of him to speak otherwise than briefly. The city of Boston being desirous of expressing its respect for the memory of Alexander von Humboldt, resolutions had been passed and a generous appropriation made, while a committee chosen from both branches of the City Government had appointed him to speak upon this occasion. In their behalf it was now his pleasure to invite all present to partake of a collation prepared for them in the hall below.

On this invitation the company cheerfully adjourned to the lower hall, to partake of the elegant repast, during which the Germania Band at intervals added their enlivening music to the entertainment.

After the company had sufficiently refreshed themselves with the delicacies of the table, the chairman invited their attention to the following poem, prepared for the occasion by Dr. Oliver Wendell Holmes.

BONAPARTE, Aug. 15th, 1769. — HUMBOLDT, Sept. 14th, 1769.

  Ere yet the warning chimes of midnight sound,
   Set back the flaming index of the year,
  Track the swift-shifting seasons in their round
   Through five score circles of the swinging sphere.

  Lo, in yon islet of the midland sea
   That cleaves the storm-cloud with its snowy crest,
  The embryo heir of empires yet to be,
   A month-old babe upon his mother's breast.

Those little hands, that soon shall grow so strong
  In their rude grasp great thrones shall rock and fall,
Press her soft bosom, while a nursery song
  Holds the world's master in its slender thrall.

Look! a new crescent bends its silver bow;
  A new-lit star has fired the eastern sky;
Hark! by the river where the lindens blow
  A waiting household hears an infant's cry.

This, too, a conqueror! His the vast domain,
  Wider than widest sceptre-shadowed lands;
Earth, and the weltering kingdom of the main
  Laid their broad charters in his royal hands.

His was no taper lit in cloistered cage,
  Its glimmer borrowed from the grove or porch;
He read the record of the planet's page
  By Etna's glare and Cotopaxi's torch.

He heard the voices of the pathless woods;
  On the salt steppes he saw the starlight shine;
He scaled the mountain's windy solitudes,
  And trod the galleries of the breathless mine.

For him no fingering of the love-strung lyre,
  No problem vague, by torturing schoolmen vexed;
He fed no broken altar's dying fire,
  Nor skulked and scowled behind a Rabbi's text.

For God's new truth he claimed the kingly robe
  That priestly shoulders counted all their own,
Unrolled the gospel of the storied globe,
  And led young Science to her empty throne.

While the round planet on its axle spins
  One fruitful year shall boast its double birth,
And show the cradles of its mighty twins,
  Master and Servant of the sons of earth.

Which wears the garland that shall never fade,
  Sweet with fair memories that can never die?
Ask not the marbles where their bones are laid,
  But bow thine ear to hear thy brothers' cry: —

" Tear up the despot's laurels by the root,
  Like mandrakes shrieking as they quit the soil!
Feed us no more upon the blood-red fruit
  That sucks its crimson from the heart of Toil!

" We claim the food that fixed our mortal fate;
  Bend to our reach the long-forbidden tree!
The angel frowned at Eden's eastern gate, —
  Its western portal is forever free!

" Bring the white blossoms of the waning year,
  Heap with full hands the peaceful conqueror's shrine
Whose bloodless triumphs cost no sufferer's tear!
  Hero of knowledge, be our tribute thine!"

After an interval the following poem, written for the occasion by Mrs. Julia Ward Howe, was read by Colonel Higginson.

Give me, O Nature, from thy summer teaching,
  A strophe for thy priest, immortal made;
Let me, too, pluck, with timid hand outreaching,
  A duteous chaplet for his regal head.

Shine out, O West! illumined by his traces,
  Ere the cramped world took notice of thy state;
He gave the record of thy virgin graces,
  And in prophetic vision saw thy fate.

Ye lifted points of flame, ye wide savannahs,
  Ye mighty streams, of mountain mothers fed, —
To you, from courtly halls and blazoned banners,
  The inner deep command his footsteps led.

Ye fair Auroras with your shafts uprearing,
　　Celestial architecture solved in light,
He knew the limits of the swift careering
　　With which you build the lofty dome of night.

O beauteous World, with wooers and adorers,
　　Eager thy favors and thy gifts to claim,
Keep thy best tribute for thy true explorers,
　　The Saints of study, reverenced in name.

And this one, from the treasury of science,
　　Where minds perplexed must pass with mystic sign,
Loosing the gates, with masterful compliance
　　Gave to the multitude her gift divine.

Thus gives the great man, — every footstep taken
　　Carries remembrance of some human need.
While the high Truth he worships, unforsaken,
　　Vouchsafes the light for which his labors plead.

No idle pomp nor futile joy delays him,
　　Sped on the earnest errands of the age;
He cannot pause when kings and courtiers praise him:
　　Too short the daylight is, too wide the page.

A paradise was his, where, trim as flowers,
　　The studious book-shelves bore the growth of thought,
A citadel of service, whose fair towers
　　Took the first message that the morning brought.

Seer of the inward vein and outward blossom,
　　Master of laws that nurture and control,
He learns, dark Mother, in thy hidden bosom,
　　The unimagined secret of the soul.

During the evening the following communications were read : —

From PROFESSOR WILLIAM B. ROGERS, *President of the Massachusetts Institute of Technology.*

"Prudence," he writes, "forbids my sharing in an occasion of so much excitement. I must content myself to keep the day at home, doing homage in my heart to the great scientific traveller, the organizer of the sciences which compose the 'Physics of the Globe,' — the Philosopher of the Cosmos, whose comprehensive learning and versatile observation have been the admiration and the guide of more than two generations of scientific explorers."

From the HONORABLE THEODORE S. FAY.

"BERLIN (Prussia), August 26, 1869.

"To the REV. R. C. WATERSTON.

"Dear Sir, — Your letter of July 29, stained but still legible, from the wreck of the Germania, came this morning. I suppose Alexander von Humboldt, as a world-intellect, ranks with Plato and Aristotle. It would be presumption in me, in the presence of such men as Agassiz, Dana, &c., to offer any particular opinion of him as a scholar. I will say a word of him as a man. It was my privilege, while Secretary of Legation in Berlin, to pass sixteen years in constant communication with him. Were I to give all my reminiscences, it would much prolong this letter. Here are two or three. I was surprised to find in so profound a thinker and scholar a continual play of almost boyish humor. He said to me one day, with an open letter in his hand, which he had just received from America, informing him that a river had been named for him: 'I wish you to know that I am a river about three hundred and fifty miles long; I have not many tributaries, nor much timber, but I am full of fish.' One summer I passed a month at Doberan, a sea-bath in Mecklenburg-Schwerin. Humboldt had addressed a letter to me there, and a word came from the legation asking whether I had received it. As I had not, I wrote him expressing my apprehension that it might be lost. The return post brought his reply. 'Do not be afraid. I wrote my name on the envelope, and I hope my fame has reached even to Mecklenburg-Schwerin.' With his humor there was a fine, not quite sufficiently repressed irony, of which I will give you one trifling example. He was present at one of our Berlin-American dinners, — I believe on the fourth of July. After many more or less brilliant speeches had been let off, his neighbor said, 'Does not this fatigue you?' He replied, 'Ach nein, ich kann sehr viel entragen,' — 'O no, I can bear a great deal.'

"He showed a singular trust that what he said would be considered confidential by all present, — so with his letters. He had a truly benevolent heart. He could never do enough for those who required his assistance, and he had a delicate sympathy, remarkable at so advanced an age and amid such absorbing occupations. The Americans at Berlin once expressed to me their desire to meet him in society. I deemed it most proper to mention this to my *chef*, who accordingly invited him, and all the Americans in Berlin. A short time after Humboldt expressed to me the wish to meet my countrymen at my house. I invited them. Humboldt was the first who arrived. He enchanted everybody by his affable conversation, and he was the very last person, late in the night, to go away.

He watched with interest the rise of eminent men in our

country, and the political course of each administration. He spoke constantly with enthusiasm of Agassiz and Dana. He was a thorough, out-and-out antislavery man, and a fearless defender of the cause of human rights in every nation. He once, with a certain degree of solemnity, intrusted to me a message to be delivered to my countrymen. 'Tell them,' he said, 'we are lost in wonder at the development of science in the United States; but we are filled with pain and apprehension at the demoralization.' I told him he did 'not understand our country: it was a battle-ground. He must not mistake a corrupt class for the people; the United States would return from their downward path and be regenerated.'

"I must cut short my *souvenirs*. I desire, however, to mention one more. I not only entertain for this illustrious person the admiration which inspires all civilized nations, but a warm, grateful, personal friendship. In one instance his friends have a right to complain that his confidence had been violated by an act more than imprudent. I have observed indications in Europe that some parties will attempt to convert the celebration of his centennial anniversary into a demonstration in favor of materialism and atheism. The endeavor to overthrow the idea of a God, now being renewed in Europe, he knew very well is as old as the tower of Babel, and as ridiculous as the attempt to build the tower that it might 'reach unto heaven.' Humboldt never favored it, and I am convinced he would frown upon any effort to identify his name with this movement. In science he confined himself to facts, and warned the student of nature not to receive even apparently demonstrated scientific systems without caution. 'Do not,' he wrote, 'confound that which is based only on imperfect induction with that which has been reduced to mathematical certainty.' He states scientific facts with impartiality and purity; and was far above the vulgar fault of leaping to conclusions because they favor preconceived theories. I once entered his room while he held in his hand a letter, which he threw upon the table with an air of indignation, saying, 'Here is a man who charges me with not believing in God.'

" I thank you for the invitation to be present at the celebration, which, of course, my temporary absence from America renders impossible. With the highest regard,

" I am, dear sir, most truly yours,

"THEODORE S. FAY."

From REV. NOAH PORTER, *Professor of Moral Philosophy and Metaphysics, in Yale College.*

" It was in the Christmas recess of 1853-54 that I saw the late Baron von Humboldt. At the urgent request of some seven or eight American gentlemen, most of them students in the University of Berlin, I addressed him a line asking the privilege of paying our respects to him in a body. To this he replied in a very courteous note, in which he expressed his gratification at the request, and proposed that we should meet him in two divisions at two successive hours. This arrangement we considered very extraordinary, and it gratified us not a little. At the hour appointed for the first division, we applied for admission at his well-known city residence, and after some delay, and as the result of some persistent explanations, we were conducted through the long suite of apartments to the reception-room which adjoined his private study. He soon appeared, and we were all struck with the peculiarities of his person. His very long and lofty head, upon a short neck, slightly inclined forward and to one side, made him appear shorter than he really was. His flesh and skin seemed very delicate and bloodless, the result of extreme old age and constant care. His person and dress were scrupulously, almost excessively neat, as became the courtier and the constant attendant upon the King. His manner towards each of us was exceedingly cordial and kind, and he placed us at once at our ease by some personal inquiries in respect to our studies and employments. We were somewhat abashed in his presence, as was natural, and our attention was divided between studying the man and suggesting the topics of conversation upon which we desired to hear him speak. We very early noticed that he talked with marvellous ease, rapidity, and fluency, and that it was only necessary to start a topic, and he was ready to discourse with fulness and fluency. His voice was exceedingly pleasant, and nothing could be more bland than his manner of expressing his always pronounced and positive opinions. The duty fell upon me, as the oldest of the company, of rather leading the conversation, but I cannot be certain that all the topics introduced by him or myself will recur to me, as I endeavor to recall them, or that those which do present themselves will occur in the order in which they were talked of.

"We spoke somewhat of his health and his habits of study and of life. He said that his uniform habit, even then, was to read till about two in the morning, and that he had rarely used, and did not then use, glasses of any kind to aid his vision. His time in the day was chiefly occupied in correspondence, in receiving visits, and in attendance upon the King, or consultation with him as Privy Councillor, and it had become absolutely necessary for him to use the hours of night for study and reading.

"In answer to some of his inquiries, or in connection with some personal remarks, I mentioned the name of the late Professor Silliman, who had visited him some two years before, and whose sketch of Humboldt, as he appeared to him at the interview, given in the Professor's most elaborate manner, had a few weeks before been copied into the papers of Berlin. In that sketch the Professor had said that the Baron had reminded him of his friend Colonel Trumbull. As soon as I spoke of Professor Silliman and the interview, he abruptly asked, 'And who was Colonel Trumbull.' I was amused at the earnestness and suddenness with which he asked the question, and was for a moment nonplussed. I happened to remember that he was once the aid of General Washington, and so replied. The answer seemed to satisfy him.

"There had been some renewed notice in the Continental papers about that time of the practicability and desirableness of connecting the Atlantic and Pacific by a canal across the Isthmus of Darien, and as this subject was introduced to Humboldt, he spoke of it with great interest and enthusiasm, and dwelt upon it at some length, described the most feasible route with great minuteness from his own personal recollections, naming every stream, pass, and place which he had traversed in person, speaking of each with the distinctness of a fresh remembrance. Nothing impressed me more than the singular power of retaining the facts and details which concerned any subject that was introduced, and in respect to no subject was this power more strikingly illustrated than in this. As he spoke, the enthusiasm of the old traveller seemed to be reawakened as he pictured to himself anew the scenery of the Isthmus which he had visited so many years before.

"He spoke of our country with great kindness, making some emphatic protests against slavery and the Ostend manifesto, which was, at that time, very fresh in the thoughts of the Europeans. He also discoursed of Mormonism, and seemed greatly to enjoy telling of the way in which two Mormon preachers had been circumvented by his counsel in their efforts to make proselytes in Berlin. These preachers, as he said, had applied to the President of the Police for permission to hold meetings, and the matter had in some way been referred to Humboldt for his opinion as to what should be said in answer. The answer which he advised was that 'the preachers would be allowed full liberty, under the laws of Prussia, to preach their religious doctrines, but that if they inculcated any practices which were criminal by the laws of the kingdom, they would be liable to arrest.' The Baron seemed to take great pleasure in telling this story, and enjoyed not a little the shrewdness of the advice by which the Mormons were circumvented.

"I took some pains to introduce the name of his brother William, knowing that he was said to hold his memory very dear, and he responded with great cordiality, and was pleased when I said that the last book which I had read before leaving home was his brother's great work upon language. This reminds me that he inquired with great earnestness and minuteness what acquaintances I had made in Berlin. When I mentioned Schelling among the number, he said that was well, and added slyly, as it seemed to me: 'He is always busy, — writes a treatise and then burns it from dissatisfaction, and then commences again.' He was too courteous, of course, to say, or even to seem to imply, that it would be well if all metaphysicians did the same.

"Another incident may seem trifling, but it illustrates one side of his character. As we were passing out through the apartments, our attention was directed to two little statuettes in porcelain of Kant and Lessing, after the originals by Rauch, which are attached to the equestrian statue of Frederick the Great. He commented upon them, preferring greatly the modest and somewhat plain figure of Kant to the studied and courtly bearing which is given to Lessing, dwelling upon the contrast at some length. He then turned to me and said: 'You must procure the statuette of Kant and take it with you to America. You will find no difficulty in carrying it. They will pack it for you at the Royal Manufactory in a little box, so that you can carry it safely in your portmanteau.' This was as we were taking our leave. We sat with him in all some half or three quarters of an hour, he, all the while, pouring forth a quiet stream of talk, which, for the gentle and rich exhilarating impression which it left, enabled me to understand, as never before, the beauty of the comparison to the falling snow which Homer applies to the words of old Nestor. He seemed desirous to detain us longer than we thought it courteous to remain, saying, when we rose to leave, that the hour had not expired, and there were many things more to talk about. When we left this dignified yet quiet abode of research and science, and emerged from the spell of his presence and his pleasant discourse into the sunlight of the gay streets of Berlin, at Christmas, we could not but feel the contrast between what was without and within.

"I write from recollection only, and have, doubtless, omitted many of the topics which were introduced, and the remarks which Humboldt made. I took no extended notes, and have not before me any entries which I may or may not have made in a diary. One of my companions may, perhaps, supply what I have omitted, and correct any error into which I may have fallen. The hasty sketch which I have made has been prepared more because I desired to show my respect for the memory of Humboldt, and my personal regard for the gentlemen who have resolved to honor it, than because the matter of it has any special value or interest.

"During the winter which I spent at Berlin I had the privilege of seeing three of the most distinguished Germans of the present century, — Humboldt, Schelling, and Carl Ritter. With Schelling I spent an evening at tea with his wife. Ritter I saw almost daily for several months, and with Humboldt I had the interview which I have imperfectly sketched. One who had seen the gray eyes of Schelling look out from his rugged and massive face could never forget them; so wonderfully glowing with fire, so active and rich in phantasy, and so penetrating with insight. It may be hard to say whether Schelling were more a poet or a philosopher, but none could deny that he was a marvellous man. In his own house he was a cheerful and playful host, full of pleasant talk and affectionate kindness. Ritter was always the same solid, sagacious, true-hearted, and all-remembering, marvellous for the facts which he had at his command, more marvellous still for his grasp of generalization, and still more wonderful for the sagacity with which he interpreted the arrangements of the physical universe by the designs of Providence, as developed in the history of man. Not the less great did he seem to me when he stood in the town church of a Christmas morning, his head towering above the multitude, and his honest face glowing with devotion as he sang with thousands the Christmas hymn.

"Of the three, Humboldt has been rightly esteemed the greatest, for the place which he filled so long, as the observer of the universe, of which man is at once the interpreter and the king. No man has served so long as he in the temple of science, as the patient observer, the daring adventurer, the curious traveller, the sagacious interpreter, and the bold prophet. None has embraced so wide a field of study and reading, and has explored it so well. None has been so ready to second and to honor the efforts of his fellow-students, — none has lived so long with so few jealousies and rivalries, — none has borne himself so courteously and humanely to his fellows. The place which was accorded to him while living, he occupied without envy; for he had no rival. The honors which are given to his memory are rendered with the unanimous acclaim of the votaries of science; for among all the students of nature in all generations there has been but one Humboldt.

"N. PORTER.

"Yale College, September 13, 1869."

From MR. JOHN G. WHITTIER.

"AMESBURY, 9th mo. 6th, 1869.

"*To* R. C. WATERSTON, JEFFRIES WYMAN, *&c., Committee:* —

"Gentlemen, — I fear I shall not be able to be present at the centennial celebration of the birth of Alexander von Humboldt, to which you invite me, but I cannot let the occasion pass without expressing my entire sympathy with the object of the society which you represent. There is little danger of overestimating the worth of such a man as Humboldt, whose reputation, outgrowing the limits of nationality and breaking down distinctions of race and language, has become universally acclimated, the common property of Science, Civilization, and Human Progress.

"What most impresses me, in contemplating his life and character, is their symmetry and rounded completeness. He was not exceptionally great in one direction only; wherever you touched him you felt the firm muscle of his intellectual strength. He saw all sides with cosmical appreciation. His mind, like the wheels of Ezekiel's vision, was 'full of eyes round about.' He had a broad, generous nature, and neither Art nor Science nor Philosophy could overlay and smother his humanity. The profoundest of all students of the laws of the universe, he was never indifferent to the welfare of his fellow-men. He hated all slavery, mental, spiritual, physical. He was only intolerant of intolerance. His generous and hearty interest in the cause of freedom in the United States can never be forgotten by those of us who, in dark and evil days, were cheered by his approval and sympathy.

"Doubtless, it is not well to set up human idols. But

while judging severely of wasted and dishonored lives, it surely becomes us to cherish gratefully and reverently those marked by noble aims and honorable achievement.

"Honor, then, to the great German, and let a common admiration of the flower and consummation of Teutonic genius and culture serve to unite in closer brotherhood his countrymen and ours.

"Very truly your friend,
"JOHN G. WHITTIER."

LIST OF SUBSCRIBERS

TO THE

"HUMBOLDT SCHOLARSHIP."

George B. Blake,	$ 500.00
Uriah A. Boyden,	200.00
William Endicott, Jr.,	200.00
Stephen Salisbury,	200.00
R. W. Hooper,	125.00
John B. Alley,	100.00
William T. Andrews,	100.00
William E. Baker,	100.00
James M. Barnard,	100.00
E. B. Bigelow,	100.00
Gardner Brewer,	100.00
Martin Brimmer	100.00
William Claflin,	100.00
John Cummings,	100.00
Francis Dane,	100.00
George B. Emerson,	100.00
Fogg, Houghton, and Coolidge,	100.00
John Gardner,	100.00
George W. Gibbs,	100.00
William Greene,	100.00
L. B. Harrington,	100.00
J. C. Hoadley,	100.00
Samuel Hooper,	100.00
F. M. Johnson,	100.00
Eben D. Jordan,	100.00

H. P. Kidder,	$100.00
Abbott Lawrence,	100.00
Amos A. Lawrence,	100.00
J. L. Little,	100.00
Mrs. J. E. Lodge,	100.00
George C. Lord,	100.00
John J. May,	100.00
E. R. Mudge,	100.00
E. B. Phillips,	100.00
George C. Richardson,	100.00
W. R. Robeson,	100.00
H. B. Rogers,	100.00
Benjamin S. Rotch,	100.00
E. F. Shaw,	100.00
Mrs. G. Howland Shaw,	100.00
D. N. Skillings,	100.00
W. B. Spooner,	100.00
George Ticknor,	100.00
R. C. Waterston,	100.00
Marshall P. Wilder,	100.00
Jacob Bigelow,	50.00
Eben Dale,	50.00
Theron J. Dale,	50.00
Charles Deane,	50.00
Charles L. Flint,	50.00
R. B. Forbes,	50.00
J. F. Hunnewell,	50.00
George B. Hyde,	50.00
George Lawton,	50.00
J. A. Lowell,	50.00
F. S. Merritt,	50.00
W. D. Pickman,	50.00
Eliza Susan Quincy,	50.00
Alexander H. Rice,	50.00
Joseph S. Ropes,	50.00
Warren Sawyer,	50.00

Joseph Souther,	$ 50.00
G. W. Wales,	50.00
C. M. Warren,	50.00
George W. Warren, Charlestown	50.00
Webster & Co.,	50.00
Henry W. Williams,	50.00
J. B. Bright,	25.00
William Monroe,	25.00
N. B. Shurtleff,	25.00
E. J. Young,	25.00
G. H. Kuhn,	20.00
S. Powell,	20.00
John Bacon,	10.00
J. M. Manning,	10.00
Thomas Gaffield,	8.00
N. Paine,	6.00
J. H. Thorndike,	6.00
S. R. Urbino,	6.00
Welch, Bigelow, & Co.,	150.00
Proprietors of the Boston Daily Advertiser,	86.38
" " Daily Evening Transcript,	54.87
" " Daily Evening Traveller,	54.75
" " Boston Post,	33.66
" " Commonwealth,	8.75
" " Christian Register,	3.30
Total,	$ 6,902.71

The HUMBOLDT CELEBRATION COMMITTEE *in account*
Dr.

By Cash received from the sale of tickets to Professor Agassiz's
    Address, ... $ 2,133.00

By Amount of subscriptions to the Humboldt Scholarship in
    the Museum of Comparative Zoölogy, as per previous
    list, . . , ... 6,902.71

$ 9,035.71

with the BOSTON SOCIETY OF NATURAL HISTORY.

Cr.

By Cash paid for Advertising: —
Boston Daily Advertiser,	$ 175.75	
Boston Post,	132.24	
Daily Evening Traveller,	113.88	
Boston Evening Transcript,	109.75	
The Commonwealth,	17.50	
Christian Register,	13.20	
		$ 562.32
By Cash paid for rent of Halls,		135.00
" " Harvard Orchestra,		270.00
" " Printing: —		
Welch, Bigelow, & Co., Address,	450.38	
A. A. Kingman, Circulars, &c.,	120.07	
		570.45
By Cash paid for sundries, postage, &c.,		34.63
		1,572.40
Balance in favor of the Humboldt Scholarship,*		7,463.31
		$ 9,035.71

* The proceeds of the sale of the Address will be added to this.

At a meeting of the Council of the Boston Society of Natural History, held November 17, 1869, it was

Voted, That the net proceeds of the celebration of the Centennial Anniversary of the birth of Humboldt, together with the money received from the sale of Professor Agassiz's Address, previous to January 1, 1870, and the money subscribed at the solicitation of the Society's Committee, be given to the Trustees of the Museum of Comparative Zoölogy at Harvard College, in trust, for the establishment of an endowment under the title of the "Humboldt Scholarship," the income of which is to be solely applied, under the direction of the Faculty, toward the maintenance of one or more young and needy persons engaged in study at said Museum.

Printed in Dunstable, United Kingdom